MW00452050

To Ted

This is your heritag

By Morris

January 5, 2009

CHARLESTON'S GREEK HERITAGE

GEORGE J. MORRIS

Charleston H London

THE
History
PRESS

Published by The History Press
Charleston, SC 29403
www.historypress.net

Copyright © 2008 by George J. Morris
All rights reserved

First published 2008

Manufactured in the United States

ISBN 978.1.59629.561.2

Library of Congress Cataloging-in-Publication Data

Morris, George J.
  Charleston's Greek heritage / George J. Morris.
     p. cm.
  Includes index.
  ISBN 978-1-59629-561-2
  1. Greek Americans--South Carolina--Charleston--History. 2. Immigrants--South Carolina--Charleston--History. 3. Greek Americans--South Carolina--Charleston--Social life and customs. 4. Greek Americans--South Carolina--Charleston--Religion. 5. Holy Trinity Greek Orthodox Church (Charleston, S.C.) 6. Greek Americans--South Carolina--Charleston--Biography. 7. Community life--South Carolina--Charleston--History. 8. Charleston (S.C.)--Ethnic relations. 9. Charleston (S.C.)--Social life and customs. 10. Charleston (S.C.)--Religious life and customs. I. Title.
  F279.C49G7 2008
  305.88'930757915--dc22
                    2008027630

Notice: The information in this book is true and complete to the best of our knowledge. It is offered without guarantee on the part of the author or The History Press. The author and The History Press disclaim all liability in connection with the use of this book.

All rights reserved. No part of this book may be reproduced or transmitted in any form whatsoever without prior written permission from the publisher except in the case of brief quotations embodied in critical articles and reviews.

Dedicated to my mother, Margaret Gazes Morris,
who instilled in me a love of history and pride in my Greek heritage.

CONTENTS

CONTENTS

ACKNOWLEDGEMENTS

The writing of this book would not have been possible without the dedication and assistance provided by Rosa P. Paulatos, who served as Parish Secretary and later Administrator of the Greek Orthodox Church of the Holy Trinity in Charleston during the period from January 1, 1954, to October 3, 1993. The Greek community of Charleston owes a debt of gratitude to Rosa for maintaining a precise history of the parish, the details of which are evident in this book.

Research material is also acknowledged to have been obtained from the excellent book by George J. Leber entitled *The History of the Order of AHEPA (American Hellenic Educational Progressive Association) 1922–1972, Including the Greeks in the New World and Immigration to the United States* (1972) and *Adallis' Greek Merchants' Reference Book and Business Guide*.

Additional information has been obtained from various program books promulgated on behalf of the church and the Order of AHEPA in Charleston commemorating various occasions in the history of the Greek community, including dedication of the Greek Orthodox Church of the Holy Trinity in Charleston in 1953. In this regard, I acknowledge Harry H. Gianaris, Jerry M. Jackis and Lucy Stupenos Spell for their efforts in documenting some of the history of the Greek community, as well as others unknown who contributed these program books.

Reference material has also been obtained from various articles published in the *Charleston News and Courier*, and some cemetery information was obtained as compiled by Mildred Keller Hood (Bethany) and Nancy Hamlin Moorer (Live Oak Memorial Gardens) for the Charleston Chapter, South Carolina Genealogical Society.

Rosa P. Paulatos was Parish Secretary and later Administrator from January 1954 through October 3, 1993.

Finally, I acknowledge the assistance of my secretary of approximately twenty years, Linda Graham; my secretary Kimberly Thomas; and my nephew John Q. Florence, who assisted in typing the manuscript for this book. I also acknowledge Margaret Eigner for assisting me with the index to the book, my daughter Nicole Morris and Magan Lyons, who assisted in compiling the pictures for the book.

INTRODUCTION

The purpose of this book is to provide a composite of the history of the Greek people in Charleston, South Carolina. As a second-generation American of Greek descent, it became apparent to me that future generations would want a better understanding of their roots in the New World, and unless my generation put this history to paper, its details would be lost, or in any event be more difficult to gather. This history is not unlike that of other ethnic groups that settled in Charleston whose histories have been documented. Most recently, for example, the Jewish community and the Irish of Charleston have taken great pains to preserve their heritage. Therefore, why not the Greeks?

First Greek Settler in Charleston and in North America

Maria Gracia Dura Bin Turnbull from Smyrna, Asia Minor, the daughter of a Greek merchant, who married Dr. Andrew Turnbull, is noted for being the first Greek female settler in Charleston County and in fact in North America, according to records of the Greek Orthodox Church in Constantinople (now Istanbul, Turkey).

Maria was born in 1736 in Smyrna, Asia Minor. She was educated in Paris, where she met Turnbull, who was studying medicine there. Maria married Dr. Turnbull in 1753. Turnbull was the organizer of an ill-fated New Smyrna Colony near what is now New Smyrna Beach, Florida.

After the Peace of Paris in 1763, England took possession of the former Spanish colony of Florida. As most of the Spanish settlers had left the colony for Cuba, the British decided to colonize the area by bringing people from the Mediterranean area, including Greeks, who were accustomed to a hot climate and were used to farming, were sober and industrious and would be happy to leave their Turkish rulers.

Dr. Turnbull secured a grant of forty thousand acres in conjunction with Sir William Duncan on the east coast of Florida with the requirement from the English government that it be settled within ten years with one person per one hundred acres. Financing his project with bounties from the government and the Board of Trade, Turnbull visited several Mediterranean ports in 1767 enlisting colonists.

Turnbull's fleet of eight ships with 1,403 colonists from Greece, Minorca, Italy, Corsica and Mahon left Gibraltar on April 17, 1768. During the long voyage, 148 died on board ship and 1,255 survived to reach their destination in Florida. Turnbull's agents in St. Augustine expected him to arrive with only 500 colonists and provisions were insufficient.

The colonists, however, survived the seventy-five-mile trip south to the site of New Smyrna, which Turnbull had named in honor of his wife's birthplace. Food was short,

Maria Gracia Dura Bin Turnbull, wife of Dr. Turnbull.

sickness was rampant and the whole area was called "The Mosquitoes" for good reason. Clouds of insects swarmed everywhere, bringing malaria to add to the colonists' miseries. By the end of the year, 450 of the 1,255 who had arrived in Florida had died. During the life of the colony (1768–77), a total of 964 persons died of starvation and sickness.

Turnbull and his partners had difficulty raising funds for the colony. The colonists had been promised freedom after four to six years of indentured service, but the colony was in such bad financial straits that the colony owners refused to discharge the colonists after the end of their service and confined them to the colony instead. After repeated petitions for freedom, conditions at New Smyrna became an open scandal in London and the colonists were released from indenture by Turnbull's attorneys. Most of the colonists left for St. Augustine and Turnbull was imprisoned for debts to his creditors in England. Mrs. Turnbull and her children apparently remained in Florida while Turnbull was in prison.

The Turnbulls came to Charles Town in 1781, after Dr. Turnbull had served his prison sentence. He died here in 1792, by that time a prominent Charlestonian. Maria died August 2, 1798, at the age of sixty-two. She and her husband are buried at St. Philip's Cemetery on Church Street in Charleston. A ceremony sponsored by the Charleston Chapter of the American Hellenic Educational Progressive Association (AHEPA) as part of the Charleston County Bicentennial Committee Founders Festival placed a plaque at her gravesite in St. Philip's Cemetery in her memory. The ceremony was attended by one of Mrs. Turnbull's relatives who lived in Charleston County. The obituary in the *Charleston Gazette* noted that during her years in Charleston, Maria had been much admired for her pleasant temperament and her grace as a lady.

On May 11, 1974, Plato Chapter No. 4, Order of AHEPA, dedicated a marble marker to the memory of Maria Gracia Dura Bin Turnbull at St. Philip's Church Cemetery. *Left to right*: Steve G. Moskos, chairman of the AHEPA Committee, and George J. Morris, president of the Chapter.

The Turnbulls' most notable offspring was Robert James Turnbull, who originated the Nullification Movement in South Carolina.

Mrs. Corita Doggett Corse's book on the New Smyrna colony, loaned to the *News and Courier* by a Mrs. Ethel S. Nepveux, gives insight into Mrs. Turnbull's character. Mrs. Corse said the young Greek woman, then thirty-three years old, played a courageous part in the New Smyrna venture.

> *She faced the dangers of the savage new land resolutely several times, ran the affairs of the settlement when business took her husband to New York or London and raised her seven children to take a creditable part in the history of Florida and South Carolina.*
>
> *...Here was indeed a life of more variety than is granted to most people of her day—to be reared in Asia Minor, to enjoy the life of London society as a young married woman, to establish her family in a wild land, beset by Indians and to end her days in Charleston, the most aristocratic city of the colonial times, as a leader there by reason of her cosmopolitan charm and her husband's high position.*

There is a National Greek Orthodox shrine known as St. Photios National Shrine located at 41 St. George Street in the old section, or "Spanish Quarter," of St. Augustine, Florida. This shrine commemorates the plight of these early Greek colonists. At the location of the shrine there was an early church founded by these colonists and a cross was found there that has been replicated and is available at the shrine. Dr. George S. Croffead, a past Parish Council President of Holy Trinity Greek Orthodox Church in Charleston, headed a committee to establish the shrine and made a significant contribution to become the "Godfather" of the shrine at its dedication in January 1985. Additionally, the Chamber of Commerce of New Smyrna Beach, Florida, has literature chronicling the history of the colony, which has been called the "Plymouth Rock" of the Greek people in the New World.

THE EARLY GREEK IMMIGRANTS OF CHARLESTON

A Mr. Young (Neos) is described in *Adallis' Greek Merchants' Reference Book and Business Guide* (which was also a general Greek directory for the City of Charleston, South Carolina, for the years 1911 to 1918) as the oldest Greek inhabitant in Charleston. The Adallis' book lists certain Greek merchants in the city, together with their families. Mr. Young could not remember precisely how many years he had been in Charleston, but he is quoted as saying that the Greeks sixty years preceding were merchants with lots of money and great influence among the Americans. He was not as complimentary toward the later immigrants in the *Adallis'* write-up, although the information provided about these immigrants reflects that they were also industrious and successful. The only disparity to Mr. Young appears to be that they were latter-day immigrants, whereas he had migrated to America years before.

These individuals and families referenced in the *Adallis'* book are some of the founders of the modern-day Greek community of Charleston. The *Adallis'* book is such a treasure of information with regard to the early Greek immigrants that it is quoted as follows for the majority of the remainder of this chapter.

EXCERPTS FROM
ADALLIS' GREEK MERCHANTS' REFERENCE BOOK AND BUSINESS GUIDE

Reports and statistics show that the Greeks are generally cash buyers, and good risks on open accounts. However, as some of them got in business with insufficient running capital, the risk to the wholesaler depends on the success of the business. It is advisable to investigate carefully the antecedents and character of the person seeking an open account.

For this purpose a CORRESPONDENT is selected in every section wherein this book is circulated, a man whose standing is good and who has known, or been in the city at least ten years. Any information the merchants who advertise in this book may desire to have, the correspondent will cheerfully give. All outside inquirers must enclose stamped envelope for prompt reply. Correspondents have no time to answer inquiries of a general character, but take pleasure to give their best attention to specific and brief inquiries. Those who are not advertising in this book are requested to remit fifty cents with each inquiry. All inquiries of a general nature should be addressed to the publisher. The ratings in this book are called after a thorough investigation. It is the sifting down, first, of personal declaration; second, report of American merchants who have dealt with them for a period of not less than two years; third, of prominent Greek merchants who know them for a length of time, either in this or in the old country; fourth, from friends and relatives; fifth, from their enemies, so may be said. All these are carefully boiled down to what we think a reliable commercial rating which we hereby give for the benefit of our friends and advertisers.

OUR CORRESPONDENT FOR CHARLESTON, S.C.

George Pharaclo was born in Lixouri-Cephalonia, Greece, and comes from one of the leading mercantile families of Greece, which is well known throughout Europe as wholesale dealers in liquors and currants. He was a law student in Athens, but owing to a small cause with his brother, who is one of the leading physicians and surgeons there, he left his home, property and everything and traveled around the world, until, finally about ten years ago he settled in Charleston and was employed by S.P. Schiadaressi as manager of the Merchants' Club, corner of King and Wentworth Streets, but owing to his business ability and knack of making friends in about a year's time he opened a restaurant and soft drink saloon on Market Street which he made a success of. Four years ago he thought farming would pay him better and accordingly went into that business, but lost everything. About two years ago he returned to Charleston and opened a small lunch counter, without hardly anything. After a few months in this business he realized a little money and opened the New York Inn, at 49 and 49½ Market street, which is a restaurant and near-beer saloon and also furnished rooms, in which place he is at present. After a few months' prosperity he took as partners, G. Magoulas and D. Koustubardi, both of whom belong to the same island and who are good quiet men who know how to make friends. As they have made wonderful progress they are going to start in the wholesale business.

Geo. Pharaclo is a big-hearted man, who is a poor man's friend and has helped many a man who had neither money or friends, and is always ready and willing to leave his business to help his friends and get them out of trouble, gratis.

He is a citizen of the United States and speaks several languages. He is a member of the Knights of Honor.

A.

Abatiello, Geo & Bros. Calhoun Street, Fruits, Soft Drinks, etc. Michael Abatiello, Manager.

ACADEMY INN 216 King Street. Phone 2821. Table and Counter Service. Nick Stratakos & Bros., Proprietors. Nick, John, James and Charles, four partners, serve as waiters; Athanasios Koumboyiannis, chief cook; Antonios Fakis, cook.

Mr. Nick Stratakos was born in Agios Nikolaos of Epidauros-Lemera, emigrating to this country in 1900. He first followed the Pan-American Exposition at Buffalo, N.Y., then to Charleston, again the St. Louis Exposition in 1904, when he returned to Charleston where he has been ever since. He runs the above restaurant in partnership with his brothers, John, Jim, and Charlie. He claims to have opened twenty-eight stores in the city. He is a full citizen, and the first Greek starting a restaurant here.

Altine, Mitchell 45 Columbus Street, opposite Union Depot. Fruits, Cigars, etc., Confectionery, Soft Drinks, Groceries and Cards.

Mr. Mitchell Altine[1] hails from Smyrna, the greatest seaport town on the Asiatic coast of the Mediterranean Sea. He is a college graduate having received his education in the American College of Smyrna. Perhaps it was a wanderlust spirit that cast him on our shores immediately after his graduation—as he would have had, no doubt, a brilliant career back there in the old country. Young men possessing his training are in great demand in these reconstruction days of Turkey. However, in 1902, he came to New York, where he was put to manage a factory for packing figs. Three years after he came down South, and at Lynchburg, Va., he managed a fruit store. At Bristol, Tenn., he launched out for himself and established an ice cream and candy factory, supplying the whole state of Virginia. He is a full citizen, a member of the Eagles, a married man with three children. He holds the office of Secretary for the Greek Community. Good, honest, and energetic. We predict for him a good future.

ANASTASH, A 373 King Street, Phone, 3909-L 5c, 10c, 25c, 50c Department Store.

A. Anastash is one of the wealthiest Greeks in the city, and one of its oldest citizens, having arrived here some nineteen years ago. He was born in Koutali, a seaport in Asia Minor, in 1865, and spent six years of his life a seafaring man. He married an accomplished Irish lady who is cooperating with him in the success of his above business. He is a full citizen and a member of the W.O.W., also a trustee of the Greek Orthodox Church, and is a man well liked by everybody who knows him.

Antonelos, Christos, 2 Anson Street, Lunch and Near-Beer Drinks. Antonelos, C., is 27 years in Charleston. He is 57 years old. Born in Lixouri, Cephalonia.

Apostolatos, Sofianos. 229 St. Phillips Street. Groceries, Fruits, Vegetables and Near-Beer.

Aseptic Barber Shop…(See C. Christopoulo.) 207½ Rutledge Avenue. No Phone. Const. Christopoulo, Prop.; Demetrios Isouloufopoulos, Barber; Louis Papas, Tonsorial Artist.

Avlihos, Marcos. 124 Calhoun St. Painting Contractor.

B.

Baltimore Lunch Room. 507 King Street. Geo. A. Panuchopoulo, Prop; Paikos Demetropoulos, waiter; Demeterios Demetropoulos, waiter; Geo. Pappas, waiter.

Baltimore Restaurant 29 Market Street. Near-Beer Drinks a specialty. Charalambos Likoudes, Prop. Three Greeks employed.

Baranno, G. Lyons Street Grocer.

Bart, Geo., 48 Archdale Street. Drinks.

Billias, John 107 King Street. Five years in the United States. Married. Born in St. Nicholas, Epidauros-Lemera.

Busy Bee Lunch Room, 449 King Street.

Busy Bee Pool Room, 449½ King Street. Artemis Poulitzakis and Pete Maroulakos, Props.

GEORGE BILLIAS

Our good friend, and ambitious young man, Mr. Geo. Billias, the Vice-President of the Grecian Society, was born in Athens. After securing a preliminary education, in December of 1906, he came to the United States. New York City was where he gained his knowledge of the English language, but Charleston has been his permanent home as he here went into business and showed his ability and made many friends, who like him very much. Courteous and congenial, Mr. Billias is an ornament to the community, so hard did he work for its progress and welfare. He brought into existence the famous Grecian Society, chartered under the State laws of South Carolina, and through it, the materialization of the Greek Orthodox Church. He is a full citizen and popular among Americans and a member of the German Suetzen Club.[2]

C.

Charleston Café, 84 Calhoun Street, East. Small Lunch and Near-Beer Saloon.
GEO. KONTOS, Prop; Nick. Karagangapoulos, help.

Geo. Kontos was born in Agrapha of Asia Minor, and has been six years in Charleston. It is said of him that he fills the same post to the negroes in his neighborhood as a scare-crow to the crows and marauding birds. Fame travels fast and wide! He is a good man though, when no one steps on his corns. Then—I really do not know.

CONSTAN H. CHRISTOPOULO 205 Rutledge Avenue. Phone 2168. Groceries, Foreign and Domestic Fruits, Bird Cages, Fish Bowls, etc.; Nicolas Christodoulopoulos, clerk, Panayiotes Constantakopoulos, clerk. Constan H. Christopoulo, 205 Rutledge Avenue, Pool Room, Ice Cream Parlor and Confectionery.
ASEPTIC BARBER SHOP. 207½ Rutledge Avenue. C.H. Christopoulo, Prop. Demeterios Tsouloufoulos, barber; Louis Pappas, barber.

Mr. Constan H. Christopoulo[3] was born in Mostitzi of Kalavrita, emigrating to America in 1904, direct to Charleston. He is one of the most progressive young Hellenes we have, and a man who will one day carve a big future for himself through his energy and perseverance. He is the Treasurer of the Board of Trustees of our community, and owns the building where he conducts his business. Such men as he are valuable assets for any town.

D.

Davis Restaurant 37 Columbus Street. Phone 1432. Counter and Table Service. W.T. Davis, Prop.; Demetrios Laskares, cook; John Demelis, cook; Louis Davis, waiter.

Davis Furnished Rooms, 137 Columbus Street. Phone 1432.

Duckas, John American Street. Phone 2243. Groceries, Fruits, General Merchandise and Near-Beer Saloon.

F.

FIAMBOLI, ANDREW[4] 347 King Street. Phone 2218. FRUITS, Groceries, Cigars, etc., Soft Drinks, etc. Nick Fiamboli and Mich Rousso, clerks.

FIAMBOLI, ANDREW 157 Broad Street. Phone 33677 ....
...........(as above) Panos Fiamboli, clerk and manager.

FIAMBOLI, ANDREW. 117 King Street. (Same line of goods as above) Geo. Fiamboli, manager.

Mr. Andrew Fiamboli comes from the historic island of Ithaca, the home of the crafty Ulysses of Homeric times. In April, 1906, he emigrated to Charleston, and in such a short period of time, and considering his ignorance of the language of the land, he succeeded to own all the above stores. He well deserves credit as he is only a young man, barely twenty-six. We wish him more success, and more stores.

Theodore Papadakos, first president of the Grecian Society.

H.

Halipiebias, Nick. 77½ Columbus Street. Shoemaker and Repairer.

HOME-MADE CANDY CO. Theo. and Dem. Papadakos, Props. "Liquid" Soda Fountain, Confectionery and Ice Cream Parlors, 345 King Street. Phone 1166. Theodosios and Demetrios Papadakos, dispensers.[5]

I.

IDEAL LUNCH ROOM 533 King Street. Lunch Room and Near-Beer Saloon.
MIKE PSARAS, Proprietor. Pandelis Psaras, cook; Dem. Mavroklis, waiter. Llion Restaurant (colored) Nicolaos Lembesis,[6] Prop. Vasilios Lembesis, waiter. Opposite Union Station.

Mr. Mike Psaras is a Chian, born in that beautiful island. A sailor for sixteen years, three years ago he struck land and settled ashore in Charleston. He owns the above business, and shows great progressiveness for a seafaring man. He has declared his intentions to become a United States citizen, a step which speaks well for him. He reads and writes fairly well the spoken language of the land, and will one day have a better success in his business. We wish him well.

K.

Kamasopoulos, Nick 212½ St. Phillips Street, Lunch Room.

Was born in Dikeli, near Smyrna, in Asia Minor, and emigrated to America in 1906. He is a full citizen, and owns a parcel of real estate. Employs Christos Cholakis as cook and waiter.

KENNESAW RESTAURANT 307 King Stret. Phone 2626. Table and Counter Lunch. **CHARLES STRATACOS**, Proprietor; Kyriakos Kyriazakos, chief cook; Evangelos Androu, cook; Triphon Karpenisiotes, waiter; Louis Papadeas, waiter.

Mr. Charles Stratacos is one of the pillars of the Greek community of this city, he was born in Agios Nikolaos of the eparchy of Epidauros-Lemeras, emigrating direct to Charleston in 1901. He spent his first six years in running a fruit store, but having had enough of that kind of business, he opened up the present store which he now owns. He is a Trustee of the Greek Orthodox Church, and has worked strenuously for the progress of his fellow countrymen. He has six children, all claiming their birth in this country, with the exception of one. He is a good father and a good man; he strives to do what is right according to his own conception.

M.

MANOS, JIM and ANAST MAVROIDES Corner Prince and Archdale Streets. Near-Beer Saloon, Cigars, Cigarettes and Tobaccos. Billiard and Pool Room. 50 Archdale Street. J. Manos and A. Mavroides, Pros.; Louis Manos, Manager.

Macro Pool Room 424 King Street. (Six Tables) Panayiotis Billias and Christ Papadakos, Props.

Maroulakos, Demetrious 445 King Street. Fruites, Soft Drinks, Cigars, etc.

Both of the above gentlemen hail from the historical grounds where ancient Sparta swayed in undismayed glory as their birthplace. Mr. Jim Manos is a full United States citizen and is affiliated with the Order of Eagles, while Mr. Mavroides has been in the United States for ten years. They own the building where they conduct their business so successfully, and are very much satisfied with their present condition.

Maroulakos, Demetrious 445 King Street. Fruits, Soft Drinks, Cigars, etc.

Maroulakos, Nicholaos 605 King Street. Fruits and Soft Drinks. Geo. Marousis, clerk.

Massinis, Gerasimos 59½ King Street. Fruits and Soft Drinks.

Morakis Antonios (Lunch) 22 Coming Street. Const. and Geo. Morakis, waiters.

Moskovakis, K., Starides, Aug., Karageorge, Geo., Props. 46 America Street (Lunch Room).

N.

New York Inn 49 Market Street. Lunch Room and Near-Beer Saloon. Geo. Faraclo (See front page of biography),[7] Dennis Custubardis, Geo. Magoulas Proprietors; also American help employed.

New York Lunch Room. 49½ Market Street. (for colored). Geo. Faraclo & co., Props.

New York Shoe Shine Parlors 277 King Street.

O.

OLYMPIA RESTAURANT Northwest Corner King and Columbus Streets. Phone 2438-J. **CHARLES MANOS** and **C. Costopoulos**, Props. Table and Counter Service, Cigars, etc. Peter Costopoulos, cook; John Myers, cook.

Tripoli Greece, claims our friend, Charles Manos, the part owner of the **Olympia**. He has been, before he settled in our city, a great traveler, having been almost all over the United States. He came from the old country in 1895 went to Chicago; nine months after to Boston, Mass.; four years after to the Buffalo Exposition; then the southern part of Kentucky, and finally, Charleston. He is a full citizen and a member of the Eagles. A very energetic young man, with a better future in store for him.

P.

PANIOTTE, ANTONIOS[8] Corner Coming and Radcliffe Streets. Phone 1232-L Fruits, Groceries, Candies, Cigars, Soft Drinks, etc. NEAR-BEER

SALOON in connection. George Nikiforakis and Michael Lavrentakis, clerks.

The President of the Board of Trustees, Mr. Anton Paniotte, our good and esteemed friend, hails from Carpathus, of the historic and magnificent island of Rhodes, where the Knights of Templars and those of St. John to and from the bloody fields of Palestine, tired or wounded in their holy war against the Saracens, returned to the shelters of this island for rest and recuperation. Mr. Paniotte has been with us since 1894, some how or other, selecting Charleston from the start. No doubt he is one of the oldest Greek pioneers of this city. He is a full citizen and owns real estate property and the building where his business is found.

PANUCHOPOULO, GEO. A. 199 King Street. Phone 1693. FRUITS, Candies, Soft Drinks, Cigars, Cigarettes, Tobacco.

PANUCHOPOULO, GEO. A. 509 King Street. Phone 2770 Home Candy and Ice Cream parlor. Alexios Panuchopoulo, manager; Geo. Avromopoulos, clerk…(See also Baltimore Lunch Room.)

Our young friend, Geo. A. Panuchopoulo, is a progressive and public spirited Hellene, of Charleston, hailing from Vahlia of Arcadia, in the eparchy of Gortynia. His arrival to America is only a matter of years, when at the age of eighteen years he aspired to cast his lot here, after traveling for awhile in New York State and Missouri, he decided to come and settle in Charleston, where he has been ever since. He owns the above businesses and conducts them successfully. He is a full citizen, and well liked by all.

Pagones, Geo. Calhoun Street.

PAPPAS Geo 376 Meeting Street. Groceries, Cages, Cigars, etc., and Near-Beer Saloon and Fruits.

Pappas, John 17 State Street, Phone 3498. Lunch Room and Near-Beer Saloon. Costas Zikos, employee.

Pappas, James 153 Calhoun Street Wholesale and Retail Peanuts.

Pavion, Michael, 428 King Street, Journeyman Carpenter.

PETERS, DENIS Corner Calhoun and Coming Streets. Phone 784. Fruits, Groceries and Near-Beer Saloon. Nick Peters, manager; Aristides Peters, clerk; James Lismas, Mitch. Kolokethas, P. Economon, help.

PETERS, Geo FRUITS, Lunch Counter, Entrance to Market. Aristides Peters, clerk.

Peters, N., Lunch Room. Spring and President Streets.

Platakes, Const., Lunch Room 155 Coming Street. Geo. Pediarites, Partner.

Potamianos, Geo., 49 Calhoun Street, Foreman.

Geo. Potamianos owns two houses and has seven children. He is rich so far as the foregoing fact is concerned. He hails from Lixouri of Cephalonia, and has been in Charleston upwards of seventeen years. He is paying now for three more houses and is a full citizen. By the time he gets through he may own one hundred more houses, in which we wish him success.

Papadakos, Theo hails from Chassi, demos Elous eparchy of Epidauros-Lemeras, nomos Laconias, in the year 1894, emigrating to America. His early years he spent in Chicago, then Cincinnati, Memphis, Tenn., and in 1897 he came to Charleston establishing with his brother Demetrious, the above business. He has two sons who work in the store. He is the President of the Grecian Society, well respected by his fellow countrymen. Besides the above he owns also the Greek-American Produce Co., of Savannah, Ga.

R.

Riverside Café Corner Market and South State Streets. Costas Siregelas, Prop. Oyster and Chop House, Corner Market and Church Streets, Cost. Siregelas, Prop. Cost. Siregelas owns the Riverside Café, on one corner, and Oyster and Chop House, on another corner. He knows, evidently, his business, as corners are worth more than "middle-of-the-blocks." He is a man well spoken of by his friends, and we trust that they do not exaggerate when they speak so many good things of him.

S.

SAVOY RESTAURANT 49 Columbus Street (near Union Depot). Phone 2796 Ko. Stratakos, Proprietor. Geo. Roussos and Costos Lekakes, cooks; Theo Yetrakes, Geo. Lekakes, Const. Constantinides, waiters.

Mr. Ko. Stratakos, the proprietor of the Savoy Restaurant, is a brother to Charles, and like him claims Agios Nikolaos as his birthplace. In 1889 he left his beautiful village and went his way towards these shores, tried his fortune in the states of New York and Philadelphia; followed the exposition in Buffalo with that in Charleston, and liking this seagate well, decided to cast anchor within its precincts. He is a full citizen, a member of the Eagles, owns lots in New Jersey, real estate in town, one house on the corner of Columbus and Hanover in Navy Yard. He is well liked and respected by his Greek and American friends for his congenial manners.

SIDERIS, NICK 49 Archdale Street. Lunch Room and Near-Beer Saloon. Phillipas Pyrovolikos. Peter Manos and John Rousso, employees.

Nick Sideris is a jolly good follow. He is a happy-go-lucky bibbler, one who cares not for tomorrow, and for whom every day alike hath its joys—and he rides over them free-heartedly, open-handedly, and without the slightest trepidation for the furtive future. Like the jug of Omar Khyyam, he bubbles in and gurgles out, a constant stream of—liquid gladness and so long as he remains satisfied, we have nothing much to say about it.

Sideris Nicholaos, Painting Contractor, 22 Coming Street.

One of the oldest Greek citizens of Charleston having been almost thirty years in the city. Married, a full citizen, poor but honest, old man Sideris is one of the ancient landmarks, figuratively speaking, of the Greek community.

SCHIADARESSI, JOHN 41 Broad Street. Phone 426 Fruits, Candies, Cigars, etc. Small Groceries, Soft Drinks.

John Schiadaressi is a cousin of Spyro Schiadaressi, and has been over thirty-one years in Charleston and is quite well known, so it is unnecessary to require the publication of his photograph here. He is a man who minds his own business and has few enemies in this world.

SCHIADARESSI, SPYRO P. (See Bradstreet) 313 King Street. Phone 32 FRUITS., West India, California and Domestic FRUITS WHOLESALE COMMISSION MERCHANT. IMPORTER of Foreign Delicacies, Fancy Groceries, etc. SOLE AGENT for Re Umberto Olive Oil, AGENT for Maillards, Lowney's and Allergrettis CHOCOLATES and CANDIES.

Mr. Spyro P. Schiadaressi, in point of years, and also in many other respects, is the leading Greek gentleman of the old and antiquated city of Charleston. Nay, with his brother Tom, he is the oldest Greek pioneer within a radius covering one-half dozen, or more, Southern states.[9] His native home is not very far from the Petra pou Kounieteh, on the rugged promontory of the Island of Cephalonia—Oh, for Lixouri, really and truly a "luxury" with its picturesque scenery, with its sun-bathed landscapes, the ozone-laden Cephalonian zephyr sweetly and continually blowing on and around your face. But, alas, the lure of the land of perpetual prosperity, the uncontrollable lust for gold that brought over here so many millions of human souls, from the four corners of the world, led also our esteemed friend Spyro to emigrate. One time, along with his brother Tom, he owned over eleven stores in this city. Had Mr. Spyro been possessed of a better ambition, he would have no doubt been one of the wealthiest Greeks for many miles around. Of course, no one knows better than he than the excellent opportunities of which he did not avail himself, which are lost and gone, or

Spero Schiadaressi, president of the Grecian Society 1914–1917 and 1921.

stopped and grasped by some one more adept than he. He is a full citizen, taking a lively interest in the political affairs as well as in the commercial development of Charleston. He has three daughters, and three grown boys, with no limit to their aspirations—that is, should any one take into his head and aspire to become a President of this glorious republic!

SPIRATO, S. 42 Market Stall
Our dear old man, S. Spirato, is another Cephalonian in Charleston. It seems that it has fallen on the lot of these robust islanders to take the lead in early emigration, as he, rounding the Cape of Good Hope on board ship as a sailor, landed in Charleston in 1880, that is, before his present chronicler had seen the light of day. A picture of him was taken years ago when he was at the height of his glory and the prime of life when blind fortune favored his enterprises—one bar and two fruit stores. Now as years impress their indelible marks upon his brow, and the hoar frost nestles on his crown, old man Spirato looks backward and sighs—but why should he—life is too short, even to sigh about. Make the best of it, the best of it, dear old man Spirato!

SMYRNA RESTAURANT. (See A. Tsiropoulos)

Sofes, Geo., 75 East Bay Near-Beer Saloon and Sailors' Boarding House.

Sofianos and Geo. Apostolatos St. Philip Street. Fruits and Near-Beer Saloon.

Stavron, Strate 647 King Street (Colored Lunch Room.)

Stavron, Strate, 645 King Street Pool Room Vasilios Stavron, Manager.

STRILAKOS, STAMATES (or Tom Crofead)[10] 57 Calhoun Street. Fruits, Candies, Groceries, etc.
STRILAKOS, STAMATES, or Tom Crofead, was born in Pylos, in Messinia, emigrating in 1907. Stamford, Conn., Salt Lake City, the home of the Mormons, and Memphis, Tenn., were carefully thrashed out before our

Tom Crofead and son George S. Croffead.

Athanas T. Tsiropoulos, pioneer of the Greek community in Charleston and president of the Parish Council 1919–20 and 1946–47.

friend decided to come to Charleston. Well, here he is, a declared citizen, a member of the Eagles, a married man, a good man. Fine!

Stavron, Athanasios Corner American and Reid Streets. Pool Room and Near-Beer Drinks.

T.

TSIROPOULOS, A. 624 King Street.

Tsiropoulos, A., 624½ King Street, Restaurant. SMYRNA POOL ROOM, 609 King Street. Phone 2398. SMYRNA RESTAURANT, 609 King Street, Phone 2398. A. Tsiropoulos, Proprietor; Christos Tsiropoulos, manager; John Stamatiades, Proprietor; Procopios Athanasion and Eleftherios Bucklas, waiters and cooks.

A. Tsiropoulos, the progressive, the young man of big ideas and ardent ambitions, hails from Koutali of the Asiatic coast of the Mediterranean Sea, or the Sea of Marmora. He arrived in 1902, spent two years in traveling the states, struck Charleston—a city good enough for him—and cast his lot. He owns the above three places, for which he worked strenuously and showed remarkable business ability. He takes the front rank whenever the progress and amelioration of the Greek community is concerned. He is connected with the Rutledge Avenue Improvement Co, which is capitalized at $50,000. He is a full citizen, and a member of the Eagles. Such young men are really valuable in Charleston, as they contribute to the material wealth and growth of the city. We wish him success.[11]

U.

UNION RESTAURANT 428 King Street, Phone 592. GEO. BILLIAS, Senior Partner. JOHN MILTON, Junior Partner. Michael Billias, chief cook; Charal Billias, second cook; Thras. Drossos cook; John Katharios, waiter; Andreas Avromopoulos, waiter.

Mr. John Milton was born in Monembasia, of the eparchy of Epidauros-Lemeras. All like Mr. Milton in the United States for his affableness and cordiality. He is only 27 years of age, has entered into conjugal relationship with an American lady, and is the proud father of a baby girl, upon whom he cherishes all his paternal affections. He is a full citizen, a member of the Eagles, and the Grecian Society. He owns part interest in the above restaurant with George Billias.

W.

WILLIAMS, LOUIS (or Angelis Panuchopoulos) 561 King Street, Phone 1706. Fruits, Candies, Cigars, etc. Near-Beer Saloon. Athanasios Anagnostopoulos, clerk.

West India Fruit Co. 626 King Street. Phone 3956. Dem. Tsiropoulos, Prop.

WEST INDIAN STORE. 239 King Street. Phone 3523 M. CRETICOS, Prop. FRUITS, Candies, Bird Seed, Cages, Cigars, Tobacco, etc. Italian Olive Oil and Spaghetti, Fancy Groceries. Antonios Creticos, clerk.

PART II.
CLASSIFIED BUSINESS SECTION

BARBERS
Aseptic Barber Shop, C.H. Christopoulo, Prop................207½ Rutledge

CONFECTIONERS
Home Candy and Ice Cream Parlor, Geo. A. Panuchopoulo, 509 King St. Phone 2770
HOME MADE CANDY CO., Theo. And Dem. Papadakos, 345 King Street. Phone 1166
Consulas, Const...541 King Street

DEPARTMENT 5c, 10c, 25c, 50c STORE
A. ANASTASH..............................373 King Street. Phone 3909-L

FRUITERERS

Abaiello, Geo. and Bros..81 Calhoun Street
Altine, Mitchell ....45 Columbus
Apostolatos, Sofianos... 229 St. Phillips
Bart, Geo. .... 48 Archdale
CONSTAN H. Christopoulo....................205 Rutledge. Phone 2168
Creticos, Peter H. ....491 King
FIAMBOLI, ANDREW ....347 King. Phone 2218
Maroulakos, Dem..445 King
Maroulakos, Nick...605 King
Massinis, Ger...59½ King
PANIOTTE, ANT. Coming and Radcliffe...................Phone 1232-L
PANUCHOPOULO, GEO. A.......................199 King. Phone 1693
Pappas, Geo...376 Meeting
Peters, Dennis..............................Calhoun and Coming. Phone 784
Peters, Geo....................................Entrance to Market
Schiadaressi, John.....................................41 Broad. Phone 426
SCHIADARESSI, S.P...........................313 King. Phone 32
Spirato, S...42 Market Stall
Strilakos, Stam..57 Calhoun
West India Fruit Co.................................. 626 King. Phone 3956
West Indian Store...........................239 King. Phone 3523

FURNISHED ROOMS

ACADEMY INN.....................216 King Street. Phone 2821
Davis Furnished Rooms..........................37 Columbus. Phone1432
NEW YORK INN.......................................49 Market
Riverside Café ....Market and State
SAVOY.................................49 Columbus. Phone 2796
Union Restaurant.....................................428 King. Phone 592

GROCERS

Baranno, Geo...Lyons Street
CHRISTOPOULO, CONST., H...............205 Rutledge. Phone 2168
CRETICOS, Geo..161 Rutledge
Creticos, Peter H..................................491 King Street
Fiamboli, Andrew.........................347 King Street. Phone 2218
PIANIOTTE, ANT..................Coming and Radcliffe. Phone 1232-L
Pappas, Geo...376 Meeting
Peters, Dennis......................Calhoun and Coming. Phone 784
SCHIADARESSI, SPYRO H...............313 King. Phone 32
West Indian Store..........................239 King. Phone 3523

Mixed. Nearly all the Fruiterers, more or less, carry staple groceries in stock.

ICE CREAM

Altine, Mitchell...45 Columbus
HOME MADE CANDY CO.......................345 King Street. Phone 1166
Home Made Candy and Ice Cream Parlor...............609 King. Phone 2770
Consulas, Const..541 King Street
Christopoulo Conet...........................205 Rutledge Avenue. Phone 2168

LUNCH ROOMS

Antonelos, Christ..2 Anson
Baltimore Lunch Room..507 King
Busy Bee Lunch Room..449 King
Charleston Café...84 Calhoun
Ideal Lunch Room..533 King St.
Kamassopoulos, Nick..212½ Phillips
Morakis, Ant...22 Coming
Moskovakis, K...46 American
Pappas, John...17 State Street. Phone 3498
Peters, Geo..1 Market Stall
Peters, N...Spring & President
Platakes, Const..15 Coming
Siregelas, Const..Market & Church
Sideris, Nick...49 Archdale
Sofes, Geo..75 East Bay
Stavrou, Strate...647 King
Tsiropoulos, A...624½ King

NEAR BEER ETC. SALOONS

Academy Inn...216 King. Phone 2821
Antonellos, Christ ....2 Anson
Apostolatos, Sofianos..229 St. Phillips
Baltimore Restaurant ....29 Market Street
Baranno, Geo...Lyons Street
Busy Bee...449 King Street
Charleston Café..84 Calhoun
Christopoulo, Const. H..................................205 Rutledge. Phone 2168
Ideal..553 King
MANOS, JIM and A. MAVROIDES......................Prince and Archdale
NEW YORK INN...49–49½ Market
PANIOTTE, ANT.....................Coming and Radcliffe. Phone 1232
Pappas, Geo...376 Meeting
Pappas, John...17 State Street. Phone 3498
Peters, Dennis..Calhoun and Coming. Phone 784
Riverside Café...Market and State
Siregelas, Const..Market and Church

SIDERIS, NICK...49 Archdale
SCHIADARESSI, S.P..................................313 King. Phone 32
Sofes, Geo..75 East Bay
Stavron, Strate...645 King
Tslropoulos, A..624 King. Phone 2398
UNION RESTAURANT.............................428 King. Phone 592
Williams, Louis.......................................561 King. Phone 1706

RESTAURANTS
ACADEMY INN.......................................216 King. Phone 2821
Baltimore Restaurant...29 Market
Davis Restaurant.........................37 Columbus Street. Phone 1432
Ilion Restaurant................................Opposite Union Station
KENNESAW RESTARUANT.................307 King. Phone 2626
OLYMPIA RESTAURANT....................King and Columbus 2438-J
SAVOY RESTAURANT.................49 Columbus Street Phone 2796
Smyrna Restaurant............................609 King Street Phone 2398
UNION RESTAURANT.............................428 King. Phone 592

SHOEMAKER AND SHOE SHINE PARLOR
Halipilias, Nick...............................77½ Columbus Street
New York Shoe Shine Parlors...................277½ King Street

MISCELLANEOUS
COTTON BROKER, Charles Young (City) (See Biography Part III)[12]
HATTER, Phillip Brown............................407 King Street
CARPENTER, M. Pavlou..............................428 King Street
PAINTING CONTRACTOR, Marcos Avlihos..............24 Calhoun

PEDDLERS—(Push Cart)
Angelotites, Theo. (Peanuts)............................153 Calhoun
Pappas, James (Peanuts)...............................153 Calhoun
Papadakes, Christ (Ice Cream)............................55 Calhoun
Halogerakis, Dem. (Peanuts)............................616 Land Street
Dem. Arth. Konialia (Fruits)............................34 Archdale
DAIRYMAN, Peter Manos..................................King Street

PART III.
LITERARY SECTION

The Greeks in Charleston
Mr. Young (or Neos), the oldest Greek inhabitant of Charleston, when asked as to the number of years he has been here could not remember precisely, but as this question recalled to his mind scenes of peculiar interest for him from

across the deep gulch of bygone days, he became reminiscent and gave me the following description of the old Greek pioneer days of Charleston.

Sixty years ago, there were Greeks in Charleston—every one of them a real Greek—a merchant with lots of money and a great influence among the Americans. We were all of us, not in fruit business—those Greeks, I mean the society Greeks, but in cotton and brokerage business. We were in those early days the ones that opened the eyes of these cotton merchants about the export trade of which they had no idea of. H'm—those days, we were Greeks and were admired and respected—all fine people—all high-class Greeks.

Mr. Young subsided all of a sudden into a meditative silence, his head bowed upon his breast, his brows contracted, as if the comparison between the Greek merchants of that early period and those who have more recently arrived were a source of infinite pain to him. I left him on the curb, patting his feeble shoulder, trying to instill the spirit of optimism into the darkening corners of his mind and reverted my attention to the new element of rugged, peasant Greeks that only two decades ago began to emigrate to America. The purpose of this book was to portray this new element, and give to their friends, the Americans, a true glimpse of their life in this country, and under what conditions or circumstances they came here; and how, a race so exceedingly different in language and manners, succeeded in carving for themselves an enviable corner, marvelous in their diligence and industry, surpassing in commercial life a great number of other nationalities more akin to the Anglo-Saxon race!

There is truly an occult meaning in this fact, if we care to read the indications and the marks they have as they climb gradually higher and higher. It is not, as Mr. Young deplored, the "high-class Greek" who can grapple the menacing horns of fierce competition for existence and through sheer force of nerve and muscle survive it. There is a volume of meaning in the biographies of all these Greeks. Coming, as they did, to a strange country, bereft of the spoken language, absolutely relying on their grim courage, they, in time, become proprietors of different lines of business, and succeed materially—it is really and truly an object lesson to many of you Americans. Could you have done as much in a strange country?

Therefore, there are in them the desirable materials which, when in the process of years will become inculcated into the character of this glorious young nation, will no doubt enhance its strength and growth.

Rugged, uncultured as they may be, yet those are the essential qualities that built up a young nation. Universal history has many such examples.

The Greeks in Charleston are increasing, and their friends, the Americans, are encouraging them, hospitable and generous as they are. Charleston, with her dear old landmarks, has preserved, in its freshness, her boundless Southern hospitality, so characteristic and so predominant in this state—especially; and the Greeks, encouraged thus, are trying their level best to merit same and show their appreciation. Mark how many of us are full fledged citizens, how many of us try to assimilate ourselves by joining different orders and organizations. We are bringing our families, or intermarrying here, a proof beyond argument, of our good intentions. We are proud to adopt this country, proud to be among a people whose chivalrous ancestors opened up this vast territory and made it habitable, and we would like to do our share.

The leading business controlled by the Greeks in Charleston is that of fruits, restaurants coming next and then saloons. There is one 5c, 10c, 25c, 50c Store, with its numerous departments, one exclusive confectionery, and a few groceries. Most of the fruit stores keep in the rear of their places a bar, and seem to make good business out of it. They all, comparatively speaking, are in fair circumstances, and far better than in some other cities near about. A great number of Greeks are members of the Order of Eagles, and maintain an organization, with its officers and board of advisors.

THE GREEK SOCIETY

Offices at 345 King Street. The officers are President, Theo Papadakos; Vice-President, Geo. Billias; Secretary, Geo. Lamas; Treasurer, Const. H. Christopoulo; Advisors, Const. Stratakos, Gregorios Panuchopoulo, John Billias, Anton Paniotte.

This organization was founded on January 10th, 1910, and has a membership of forty-two. Its scope involved is the establishment and maintenance of a Greek Orthodox Church, and also the keeping of the national feeling aflame in the hearts of the backsliders. It has achieved its purpose as is evidenced by the purchase of the site valued at $750.00 and its appropriation to the building fund the sum of $4,000.00. The church is now complete, is of Byzantine style, on the corner of St. Philip and Fishburne Streets.[13] George Lamas, the youngest of the group, has a remarkable endowment of observation, and a deductive mind. As mentioned, he acts as Secretary to the above society. He was born in Issari, of the eparchy of Megalopholis, onomos Arcadias, and is only 23 years old. His sojourn in the United States dates from 1903, and the Greeks are fortunate to have a young man of his intelligence and character.

THE GREEK PASTOR

Rev. Joacheim Georges is one of the pioneer priests, having come to America eleven years ago. His first call was in Charleston, where, after officiating for awhile, he accepted a call in Lowell, Mass., striving hard to enthuse the numerous Greeks over there to build a church. The Greek Orthodox Church of Lowell is one of the most magnificent church buildings in America, with its $100,000 structure, its gilt dome, and marble cupola, all speaking loudly of the vast energy Rev. Joacheim put into the work. He again, after so long a period of years, wished to be among his first flock, and therewith came among us and co-operated with the Grecian Society for the materialization of our present church edifice. Much honor is due him, and he deserves the love the radical portion of the Greeks have for him and for his estimable co-operation and fatherly counsels.

A FRIEND OF THE GREEKS

The Greeks, although dissimilar in many respects to the Italians, yet have a warm feeling of friendship for them, and in Charleston especially we have a few Italian friends who have been in deed and in need, true and staunch friend to us. Mr. Chicco never for a moment ceased to be a friend, counselor, a father to the Greeks and in return he commands a warm corner in every Greek heart. He is, like some, one of the ancient landmarks or "human marks" of the dear old Charleston. Here he saw the prime of his life gradually cooling down with the coming shadow of years. Here, his fiery, ardent Italian nature, softened down as time kept stealing a march over him, leaving its indelible marks on his heirs. We like old man Chicco and who does not? One has to have a minute's conversation with him—then all is over, he has crept into your heart, and you can not help esteeming him highly.

THE GREEK FAMILIES

As an illustration of the magnitude of the Greek Community of Charleston, I am presenting to our American readers a few of our Greek family groups, so that the true meaning of my foregoing explanation should be more readily comprehended or appreciated. Here is a list of them, with their wives and children.

MR. AND MRS. MITCHELL ALTINE, Eugenia and Gust, children.

Mrs. Altine is an American lady, a meet companion of her husband and a happy and proud mother of three children. Good housewife as she is, yet she, like most of the wives who are anxious for the material success of their other-halves, is always found courteously waiting on customers in the store opposite the Union Depot.

MR. AND MRS. JOHN BILLIAS AND DAUGHTER, residence, 107 King Street.

MR. AND MRS. DENNIS PETERS, (a/k/a Ferentinos) residence, Calhoun and Coming Streets. Pano, and one baby, born in Charleston. Parents both natives of Greece.

MR. AND MRS. POTAMIANOS, residence, 49 Calhoun Street. Seven children, all born here, Anastasios, Maria, Annie, Tereza, Margarita, Antonetta, Jim (see biograph). "Kai tou hronou."

MR. AND MRS. A. ANASTASH. Residence, 737 King Street.

Mrs. Anastash is a rare business woman possessing the qualifications that go with it. She is the right hand of her husband and can be seen every hour of the day in the store busily engaged in satisfying the demands of the store's numerous customers. She is a typical Irish lady gentle and good hearted, so characteristic of the children of the Emerald Isle.

MR. AND MRS. SPYRO P. SCHIADARESSI, residence 266 King Street. Six grown sons and daughters, all natives of Charleston; all married but one daughter. Parents both natives of Cephalonia, Greece.

MR. AND MRS. NICHOLAOS SIDERIS, residence, 22 Coming Street.

MR. AND MRS. ALTINE Residence, 79 Bay Street

MR. AND MRS. JOHN DUKAS, residence 55 America Street. This busy man has by three wives nine children, majority grown and married. Let us enumerate; Angelos, John, Jr., Constan, Elene,—each one child; Andrew, George, Tommy, Katerina and Mary, full grown.

MR. AND MRS. STAMATES STRILAKOS (or Tom Crofead) residence, 57 Calhoun Street.

MR. AND MRS. CHARLES STRATACOS. Residence, 307 King Street

One-half dozen children; Panayiotes, Christina, Merope, John, Vasilios, Chrisoula. Excepting one, all were born here. Parents, natives of Greece. The picture conveys the impression that these fortunate parents have their arms full, though the parental and maternal pride, God's blissful reward, is so strikingly reflected from their faces. We wish them "Kai tou hronou."

MR. AND MRS. SPIRATO, residence, 199 King Street. No children.

MR. AND MRS. JOHN MILTON, John and King Streets. Mrs. John Milton come from Elloree, Ga. They are the happy parents of one sweet baby girl.

MR. AND MRS. LOUIS PAPADEAS, residence 216 King Street (newly married)

MR. AND MRS. GEORGE PETERS, (a/k/a Ferentinos) Charleston, S.C. U.S.A.

NICK STRATAKOS AND SISTER, residence, 216 King Street

MR. AND MRS. JOHN LEAS, live 71 Market Street. Both from Marion of Kynourias; have two children, Demetrios and Panayiotes.

Others are coming gradually with their wives and children; others are sending for them; some go prospecting for, others arrange matters mail-order fashion; while there is a decided tendency towards racial intermarriage,[14] as evidenced above. Whatever the case may be, the Greek community is getting ramified by the gradual increase of families. And no one can realize better than the writer that a colony or community in an isolated condition, deprived of close female companionship, and the happy sight of wee, tiny tots, or growing youths, soon deteriorates, after experiencing the brutalizing effects of such isolation. Furthermore, they cannot draw the respect of their neighbors, or enter into social life, nor can be revitalized as long as they lack the inspiring presence of the fair sex. The Greeks are realizing this fact; they are changing their original program or determination. They are gradually learning to regard this country as the best in the world, and in as much as their material prosperity begins in this country, the idea of amassing enough and going back to enjoy it is steadily and effectually disappearing.

TO OUR FRIENDS—THE ADVERTISERS

Sometimes it is a business policy not to refuse to take a space in a publication gotten up by a body of people with whom one has commercial relationship. To refuse, it is a bad policy; it prejudices your business, although the same people may continue dealing with you, yet their knowledge of the fact of your refusal and yours, creates a not very congenial contrast—and their thought of this fact certainly does your business and yourself more harm than you can realize. You should know that our thoughts are all forces towards good or evil. Your actions are influenced by the thoughts of others—and in brief, the more friendly thoughts you can draw from the people to your business, the more prosperous you will grow, and vice versa.

Some of those on whom I called, and whose names are conspicuous here by their absence, have been extremely selfish in spending five dollars, often, with the friends of their store, and others showed no hesitancy in manifesting their glaring lack of courtesy, which after all, is due, or would be given the representative of his store's friends and customers. I will mention no names, but I beg to point these gentlemen the foregoing paragraph and its occult truth to remember.

There have been others, also, grudging in their proclivities, yet apprehensive of the likely consequence of a refusal, adopting the method of "come-and-see-me-tomorrow-or-the-next-day." As a remedy, and repeating the same formula every time you go to see them. I once saw a legend hanging in a conspicuous place in an Oriental store, years ago, it said:

"To-day cash, to-morrow on credit," or
"Pay cash to-day—We credit you to-morrow."

Of course to-morrows never come, but the gullible man wastes his hopes and efforts in vain looking for that to-morrow. THEY HAD NOT STAMINA TO SAY—"NO!" They simply dodged about.

But the strangest part of it all is the inimical attitude of the "Joint Committee" of the Retail Merchants Association and Ad Club. They tried to taboo, suppress, coerce, censure, and stamp out the publication of this book. Three clerks—not employees, not merchants, NOT business men, but clerks, assumed the right to know what is good and what gives indigestion to the commission merchant, or to a retail ice or coal dealer. From mere arrangers of advertising copies, they became supreme arbiters, the bulworks and protectors of the much persecuted and heavily taxed merchants of Charleston.

About four o'clock one afternoon, I was summoned to appear before the "joint committee," to plead my cause. I did so, accompanied by the committee's secretary into a furniture store, and by a freight lift, up to the third or fourth floor, full of junk, beds and mattresses, one of which fortunately, was ready on hand to serve as "joint conference" divan. Upon the roof, odorous top did we perch and began the session. I explained, argued, tried to show what it was, but for goodness sake, no amount of argument could make an impression on the stubborn minds of three prejudiced clerks who had made up their minds beforehand.

I have no malice against them, in fact, I like them for the peculiar stand they took in "giving their decision," but I can not help feeling sorry for the august body of shrewd, self-reliant-in-some-respect, self-assertive merchants for intrusting their business management—a vital part of it— into the hands of their paid clerks, who know more about a flourish to the letter B, than Beans.

Circular letters were sent broadcast to warn them to look out for me and uphold their decision. Undaunted by such proceedings and having the whole of my people to encourage me in my endeavors, I worked strenuously, forgot in my daily rounds the threatening letters, forgot the prejudices, and finally, the present volume speaks in a measure of my success and of the good-hearted, generously-disposed, fearless friends who came forward to give me a helping hand, the glad hand of welcome and encouragement.

Nothing can defeat a self-reliant person, my courage was begotten by the latent moral purpose of this book, and it is no petty sentiment, after all is said and done. My ambition was to show my people in a true light. Here we have a deserving element, crude though as it may be, yet an element who will in days to come leave its vestiges deep in the character of this nation.

What did Young say about them—his own blood—an ignorant looker-on will say with many more additions. And it is high time now that we should amend matters and make ourselves known a little. For it is natural if you do not know a person, you take no interest in what becomes of that person. We want you to know us, and if you can, if you are a true-born American, a home-loving citizen, give us a helping hand to become real good citizens of the country we have adopted. So much for it.

Now let us come to our fearless, honest, sincere friends. What about them? Oh, to an appreciative mind, they are in this world, harbingers of hope and courage, of good will and life. World without them would have been a scene of brutality and selfishness. They are the "salt of the earth," tolerant, unprejudiced, believing in living and letting others live. Look through the book, their advertisements speak of their heart—policy or no policy—there they are, like torches aflame.

I have seen Paul Trouche, had a talk with the young energetic, ambitious cashier of the Citizens' Bank, shook hands-heartily-with Kohnarrens, the bottler, looked square at Heins & Lesemann, smiled with Robinson, the producer, all good at heart, full of frank good wishes, giving me the proper stimulas to forge ahead and over the circular letters strewn, like Chinese funeral slips, on my way. All these and for all those who manifested their friendly spirit, I have a deep sense of gratitude, for to them I owe the success of this book. Thank you all!

Dio Adallis

ADVERTISERS IN ADALLIS' BOOK

1. The Peoples' National Bank
R.G. Rhett, President, E.H. Sparkman, Vice President, E.P. Grice, Cashier

2. C.L. Kornahrens Bottling Works
196 East Bay Street
Charleston, South Carolina

3. The Citizens Bank
265 King Street
Charleston, South Carolina

4. C. Bart & Company
Wholesale Dealers in Fruit and Produce
Charleston, South Carolina

5. F.W. Wagener & Co.
Wholesale Grocers, etc.

6. C.W. Parham Co.
Fruits and Produce
82 and 84 Market Street
Charleston, South Carolina

7. J.N. Robson & Son
Commission Merchants
Fruit and Produce
136 East Bay Street

8. Vincent Chicco
Macaroni, Cheese, Olives, Olive Oil and All Italian and French Delicacies
83–85 Market Street
Charleston, South Carolina

9. Welch & Eason
The Quality Shop
Market and Meeting Streets

10. The Tiedman Company
Wholesale Grocers
172–174–176 East Bay Street
Charleston, South Carolina

11. Consumers Coal Co.
Joe P. Devenux, President
T.D. Lanigan,
Superintendent
J.H.C. Wulbern, Vice-
President
Frank P. Walsh, Secretary
and Treasurer
Office Central Wharf
Charleston, South Carolina

12. Charleston Market
250 King Street
Charleston, South Carolina

13. J.S. Pinkussohn Cigar,
Co.
Charleston, South Carolina

14. The Germania Savings
Bank
34 Broad Street
Charleston, South Carolina

15. Livingston
Two Stores: 366 King Street
Near Calhoun, S.E. Corner
& Market Streets
W.F. Livingston, Prop.

16. W.B. Whaley & Co.
Wholesale Produce
104 Market Street
Charleston, South Carolina

17. Puckhaber Bros. Co.
Manufacturing
Confectioners and Bakers
464 and 466 King Street
Charleston, South Carolina

18. The Ideal Laundry
King and Burns Lane

19. Charleston Pepsi-Cola
Bottling Company
J.T. Oglesby, Prop.
80 Market Street
(Frees the nerves and aids
digestion, refreshes, and
Invigorates)

20. Ice Delivery Company
General Office
Up-Town Office
172 Church Street
28 Wolfe Street

21. The First National Bank
John C. Simonds, President
Louis D. Simonds, Vice
President
Dwight Hughes, Cashier

22. The Bay Fruit Company
C.H. Wilburn, President
H. Hass, Secretary
H. Hirschmann, Treasurer
182 East Bay Street
Charleston, South Carolina

23. Charleston Fruit Company, Inc.
92, 94 & 96 Market Street
Charleston, South Carolina

24. C.D. Kenny, Co.
Teas, Coffee, Sugars
E.A. Pfaehler, Manager
S.W. Corner King & Liberty
Street, Charleston, S.C.

25. Fincken-Jordan, Co.
Wholesale Grocers
Charleston, South Carolina
Warehouse on Charleston
Terminal Co. Tracks.
195–197–199 E. Bay Street

26. E.F.A. Wieters
Wholesale Grocer
Nos. 178, 180, and 183 East
Bay Street
Charleston, South Carolina

27. The Dime Savings Bank
280 King Street
Charleston, South Carolina

28. The Marjenhoff Co.
Candies
30–36 Market Street
Charleston, South Carolina

29. Daily Lunch Biscuit C-
B-W
Charleston Biscuit Works
30–36 Market Street
Charleston, South Carolina

30. J.N. Schroder
Importer of Havana Cigars
and Dealer in Domestic
Cigars
219 Meeting Street, Opposite
Charleston Hotel
Charleston, South Carolina

31. Walter C. Long Signs
90 Market Street

32. Electric Supply Company
T.A. Brookbanks, President
& Treasurer
S.E. Welch, Vice-President &
Secretary
Engineers and Contractors

155 Meeting Street
Charleston, South Carolina

33. I.G. Dixon, Jr.
Stationer and Paper Dealer
299 East Bay Street
Charleston, South Carolina

34. F.W. Meyer & Son
188 East Bay Street
Charleston, South Carolina

35. Charleston Fish and
Oyster, Co.
Successors to Charles C.
Leslie
18 & 20 Market Street

36. Heins & Lesemann, Fruit

37. Zero-Cola

38. Paul E. Trouche
Wholesale
215 Meeting Street, Opposite
Charleston Hotel
Charleston, South Carolina

39. Sottile Brothers
Charleston, South Carolina
Ad Reads: "Deeply
appreciating the many favors
shown us by the Greek
residents of this community,
we wish them utmost success
in their laudable efforts."
"Our appreciation of their
true worth, as men of business
affairs and loyal citizens of
their adopted country is
based on our past convictions
and long experience."

[END EXCERPTED TEXT]

THE CORNER GROCERY STORE

During the 1930s, the 1940s and for a time thereafter, there were many Greek merchants operating corner grocery stores. In fact, there were two commercial societies of such businesses existing in 1934. One such society was the Home Grocers. Participants were as follows:

George D. Bazakas	Summerville, South Carolina
Nick J. Bazakas	North Charleston
Peter P. Botzis	southwest corner Nassau and Lee Streets
James P. Demos	133 Queen Street
D. Diasourakis	northwest corner Columbus and Aiken Streets
Nicholas H. Gianaris	northwest corner Rutledge Avenue and Spring Street
Nick S. Kaleondgis	131 Wentworth Street, later operated by a son-in-law, Peter J. Alvanos
George Kristakis	southwest corner Ashley Avenue and Bogard Street
William D. Lefter	208 northeast corner President and Line Streets, later location 182½ Coming Street
S.T. George	59 Coming Street
A. Logothetis	northeast corner Rutledge Avenue and Moultrie Street
Antonios Magoulas	northeast corner America and South Streets
George J. Morakis	northwest corner Cannon and St. Philip Streets
Jerry M. Moskos	47 Columbus Street, later operated by sons Ross, George, Marko and Constan
J.C. Palassis	northeast corner Chapel and Alexander Streets
T. Poupalos	southeast corner Meeting and Reid Streets

Another commercial society of grocery store owners, known as United Food Stores, had twelve stores:

Nicholas D. Anthony	Smith and Radcliffe Streets
Mike Fergos	Cannon and President Streets
Gongos & Pappas	southwest corner Columbus and Aiken Streets
George C. Kanellos	Cannon and St. Philip Streets
John/Spero Liatos (brothers)	485 Meeting and Columbus Streets—family grocery
George Misoyianis	172 Spring and President Streets
G. Misoyianis	southwest corner St. Philip and Cannon Streets
Constantinos (Gus) G. Moskos	Charles and Beaufain Streets

Anastasios S. Palassis	Coming and Duncan Streets
Rose C. Palassis	84 Calhoun Street
John M. Rousso	Rutledge and Race Streets
A. Stefanatos	northeast corner Sires and Bogard Streets

Among other grocery stores were the following:

Jerry E. Aliprantis	Folly Beach Road, also a fisherman
Altine Grocery	Folly Beach
Andrew G. Andreatos	Morris Street near Felix
Zesomo Andreatos	King Street near Line
Athanasios G. Anagnostopoulos	55 America Street
Costa P. Ardavanis	75 Fishburne Street
Jerry Athanasatos	53 Bogard Street
Nick J. Bazakas	215 Rutledge Avenue
Jerry Bouzos	32 Calhoun Street
Andrew J. Carabatsos	626 Rutledge Avenue
George J. Carabatsos	510 Rutledge Avenue
Angelo J. Castanes	19 Franklin Street
Chris J. Castanes	201 King Street
John T. Chakeris	132 Spring Street
Pindaros Chrisanthis	81 Coming Street
Pete and Harry Chrisantou (brothers)	Meeting and Tradd Streets
Nick J. Christopoulou	209 Rutledge Avenue
Augustine C. Chrysostom	31 Elizabeth Street, Costa's Cut Rate, previously owned by Costa Servos
Dennis Christofal	Bogard Street
Cockinos Brothers	209 King Street
Constantine M. Cockinos	59 Coming Street, New Deal Grocery
Nicholas Columbis	353 King Street

Opposite top: Pete and Harry Chrisantou's store as originally existing across from First Scots Presbyterian Church.

Opposite bottom: Mayor J. Palmer Gaillard Jr. on the far right and the Chrisantou brothers, who operated a grocery store across from St. Philip's Church on Meeting Street. The brothers are receiving a presentation from the mayor, May 1966.

Peter/Anthony Creticos (brothers)	129 Rutledge Avenue
Nicholas H. Corontzes	49 Beaufain Street
Peter D. Demetre	81 Cannon and Smith Streets. Originally opening under his given name of Prodromos Demetriou, he later anglicized and shortened his name, as was the case with many immigrants. Purchased the store in 1930 from Antionas Constandanos, who opened it in 1922.
Anastasios M. Derdelis	84 America Street
Gregorie J. Diasourakis	Line and King Streets
Nicholas J. Drake	129 King Street
Leon J. Drake	Corner of King and Tradd Streets
Angelo Drakos	Coming and Bull Streets
Stavros I. Ferderigos/ Spero J. Fokas (brothers-in-law)	Line Street
Pano D. Ferentinos (Peters) Grocery Store Later filling station	Meeting Street Road
Tom A. Fergos	176 Line Street
Chris D. Gazes	King and Cannon Streets. Later operated by Pericles Stamatiades
Theodore H. Gianaris	Calhoun and Coming Streets
Nicholas Gongos	69 Columbus Street
James D. Grevas	Cooper Street
Tony Hadgi	Huger Street near President Street
George C. Hitopoulos	168 East Bay Street
Charles Horton	572 Meeting Street
James/Frank Kordonis (brothers)	Meeting and Columbus Streets
Karapiperis	Cannon and Coming Streets
Christo N. Lambrakos	Fishburne and St. Philip Streets
George N. Latos	318 Meeting Street
Michael A. Lavrentakis	399 Rutledge Avenue, "Quality Fruit Store"
Frank E. Lawandales	460 Meeting Street, "Consolidated Grocery Store"

Flora Pepergias Lempesis	Spring Street
Nicholas P. Lempesis	1 Council Street
William P. Lempesis	45 Columbus Street
Peter P. Leventis Sr.	34 Market Street, Gulf Fruit Co. Wholesale
Angelo Logothetis	Rutledge Avenue and Moultrie Street
William J. Logothetis	1082 King Street, Rose Garden Grocery
Milton S. Magoulas	305 King Street
George G. Manos	St. Philip and Morris Streets. Later operated by Peter Morfesis
Louis Manos	269 Coming Street
James C. Manos	22 Coming Street, liquor store
Gust G. Moskos	49 Archdale Street
Frank H. Panegeris	491 King Street, fruit stand, later cigar store
James Panos	117 King Street
Pete M. Paulatos	120 Meeting Street, L&P Grocery.

Prior to L&P Grocery, 120 Meeting Street, in the early 1930s, was the location of O.K. Barbeque Restaurant, with Pete Michael Paulatos as proprietor. He is pictured behind the counter in a suit. Pictured sixth from right is Augustine (Stino) J. Augustine. Mary Klonaris Augustine is pictured fourth from the right; his wife, Lucile Sirmas Paulatos, is third from the right; and Kiki Sirmas Pappas is second from the right.

Pete J. Pavlatos	55 America Street
John D. Poupalos	Folly Beach
Evangaelia Zoumis Psaras	Riverland Terrace, Psaras Grocery
Schiadaresis Grocery	Meeting and Wentworth Streets
Costa Servos	basement George and St. Philip Streets, later John and Elizabeth Streets, Costa's Cut Rate
George J. Speliopoulos	218 Rutledge Avenue
Jerry A. Spetseris/ Chris A. Zecopoulos (brothers-in-law)	Folly Beach, Chris & Jerry's
Perry N. and John Stamatiades (brothers)	571 King Street, Stamatiades Brothers Fruit Store
George Stamos	Meeting and Columbus Streets, later owned by Frank Kordonis
Demetrios T. Stratos	251 Ashley Avenue
John J. Stratos	36 Blake Street
Milton D. Stratos	Line Street and Ashley Avenue, later real estate agent, Rutledge Avenue
Andrew A. Trapalis	86-A King Street
Charles P. Trapalis and Harry (Bobby) Trapales (father and son)	175 King Street, Charlie's Delicatessen
Andrew Tumboli	353 King Street
James G. Xenakis	41 Morris Street[15]

Many of these small business entrepreneurs not only ran grocery stores at their various locations, but also included other businesses at the same location. For example, C.D. Gazes also operated a liquor store at his location. Peter D. Demetre operated various enterprises, including a liquor store, ice cream parlor and dry cleaner, at his location on Cannon Street. The grocery stores and other businesses operated by these Greek immigrants reflected their independent spirit and their faith in our country's free enterprise system. Many of the sons and daughters of these corner grocers and the children of other business owners, such as restaurateurs, became formally educated and presently occupy positions in the business community and in the various professions.

These corner grocery stores provided personalized service to the customers and also served as social meeting places. Over-the-counter beverages and snacks would be dispensed in a familial atmosphere. It is hard to imagine nowadays that so many small grocery stores could coexist, but it should be remembered that at the time there were no supermarkets. Beginning in the 1950s, as supermarkets and convenience stores came into vogue, most of these grocery stores ceased to exist. Other ethnic groups also operated these types of stores, but it seems that the Greeks "cornered the market."[16]

RESTAURANTS

William J. Anagnos	155 Meeting Street
John Augustine	Hampton Restaurant
Spero Canalis	488 King Street, Sunrise Café
Michael D. Carosatos	Yacht Basin Snack Bar
Charles Costopoulos	377 King Street, King's Restaurant
Angelo G. Drakos	Market Street. Later purchased Anagnos Restaurant, 155 Meeting Street
Stanley E. Georgeo	foot of the Ashley River Bridge, Fork Restaurant
Demetrius K. Gionis	349 King Street, Garden Grill
Tom S. Haley	Upper King, Tower House Restaurant
George C. Hitopoulos	168 East Bay Street
Emanuel M. Houllis	333 King Street, Princess Sweet Shop
Angel G. Kettas	337 King Street, King's Restaurant
George Theodore Kiriches	629 King Street
Pete N. Lempesis	481 King Street Pete's Restaurant, later operated by his brother Gus
William J. Logothetis	1327 King Street
George J. Manos	498 Meeting Street, Manos Restaurant
George Marcos	Uptown Restaurant
Andrew (Andy) L. Melissas	Meeting Street, Andy's Hickory House
Arthur A. Pappas	615 King Street
Demos P. Pappas	621 King Street, Olympia Restaurant (partner, Angelo Stoucker)
Thomas G. Pappas	633½ King Street
Pete M. Paulatos	120 Meeting Street, OK Barbecue. Later L&P Grocery/ Liquor Store
Nick Stratakos	216 King Street, Academy Inn (partners with brothers John, Jim and Charles), Seven Seas Restaurant, King Street
Stamates Strilakos (Crofead)	next to Francis Marion Hotel, Mayflower Restaurant. Later purchased by Speros P. Poulos and named Normandy Restaurant (cook: Louis Mandas). Later purchased by John Saks, who also ran the Oyster Bay Restaurant

James A. Tellis	75 George Street
John Tjovaras	Stardust Restaurant
Harry P. Trapalis	227 Rutledge Avenue
Nick S. Tsurutis	91½ Society Street
Alex G. Tumboli	diner/ship chandlery
Pete S. Vallis	222 King Street
Mike J. Ventros	426 King Street
Varvounis Voutsas	391 King Street, Mexican Grill Restaurant
James G. Xenakis	41 Morris Street

LIQUOR STORES

George D. Bazakas	Summerville, SC
Harry P. Demos	389½ East Bay Street
Peter P. Demos	2 Broad Street
Leon J. Drake	87 Broad Street
Paul J. Efstathiou	221 Cannon Street, Greek School teacher
Chris Giaffis	Dual Lane Highway
Theodore H. Gianaris	194-A Calhoun Street
Demetrius K. Gionis	Calhoun Street
George T. Savvas	509 King Street
George A. Telegas	150 King and Queen Streets, liquor store/cigar store/candy shop

OTHER BUSINESSES

Nicholas D. Anthony	43 Market Street, sold paper goods, cigarettes, etc. to merchants
James S. Arcouzis	417 King Street, barber
Emanuel B. Banis	4044 Rivers Avenue, Siesta Motel
Pete E. Banis	3844 Rivers Avenue, shoe store
Elliott P. Botzis	689 Rutledge Avenue, pharmacist
John C. Chrysostom	Folly Beach, drugstore, Greek School teacher; now operated by his son Paul
Augustus E. Constantine	139 Calhoun Street, architect (designed Hellenic Center on Race Street). Location later Tavern on the Green, operated by Jerry M. Jackis.

Nicholas H./ Theodore N. Garbis (father and son)	43 Market Street, wholesale candy and cigar shop
Demetrius K. Gionis	hat cleaning
George C. Gonos	496 Rutledge, George's Shoe Repair
Menelaos Geo Jackis	barber
Christopher John Kyras	Cleveland Street, tile company
Pano A. Lamis	239½ King Street, Boston Hat Cleaner
Sam M. Latto	4355 Dorchester Avenue, later 727 King Street, Canada Dry Bottling
Peter W. Lempesis	45 Columbus Street, Royal Dry Cleaners
George Nicholas Leussis	16 Market Street, Fish Market
Emmanuel G./Koula B. Malanos	Highway 61, later moved to Calhoun Street, florists
John B. Marcus	8 Broad Street, pharmacist
Michael J. Mellis	cabinetmaker
Nicholas J. Michaelidis	628 King Street, Harmony Drive In
Pete N. (Papaphilippou) Philipps	207 Spring and Chinquapin Streets, candy store and wholesale
John N. Pieracacos	371 King Street, Johnny's Newstand (later Francis Marion Restaurant)
Steve/Emanuel S. Redman (father and son)	121 Spring Street, Charleston Pressing Club
Panagiota, Maria, and Ted N. Stratakos (mother and children)	Hampton Park, snack stand
James A./Anthony (Tony) J. Tellis (father and son)	125 King Street, soda fountain, drugstore, pharmacy; now operated as Tellis Pharmacy by sisters Vera J. Tellis and Alice Tellis Critikos
Nicholas G. Theos	life insurance underwriter
Athanas T. Tsiropoulos	607 King Street, Try-Me Bottling Co.
Theodore C. Varvalides Varras	401½ King Street, Carolina Drug Store
Pete A. Yatrelis	123 West Richardson Avenue, Summerville, general store; later Continental Corner Restaurant, operated by his son Father Ernest P. Yatrelis and partner Tom Mavrides

The Greek Orthodox Church of the Holy Trinity and the Charleston Greek Community

Church History

In 1908, the first Greek Orthodox church liturgy in Charleston is recorded to have been performed in St. John's Episcopal Church at the corner of Amherst and Hanover Streets by the Reverend Arsenios David of Savannah, Georgia. Subsequently services were held at a house at the corner of Calhoun and Coming Streets by the Reverend Ioachim George.

In 1909, a group of approximately fifty Greeks gathered at 345 King Street, home of Theodore Papadakos, and organized the Parthenon Society, with Papadakos as president.[17] Family names from this time included Lamas, Panoutsopoulos, Davis, Demos, Rousso, Lempesis, Christodoulopoulos, Stratacos, Billias and Milton. Some of their descendants are members of the Greek community of Charleston to this very day. The following year, 1910, the Grecian Society of Charleston was formed, with the organizational meeting held at Carpenter's Hall located on Vanderhorst Street in the city.[18]

The Certificate of Incorporation for the Grecian Society on June 15, 1910, states that Theo Papadakos, George Billias and John Billias of Charleston did apply for incorporation of said society for religious, social, fraternal, charitable or other eleemosynary purposes. The purpose of the corporation was stated as follows: "The alleviation and the protection of our brother Greeks' suffering, and the maintenance of our Country and Religion, the Orthodox Greek Catholic Church." The names of all managers, trustees and directors or other officers were listed as Theo Papadakos, president; George M. Billias, vice-president; John Billias, secretary; and Constan Christopoulo, treasurer. The Grecian Society and other like societies organized in other cities by Greeks brought priests to America, establishing the Greek Orthodox Church in the New World, and also acted as benevolent societies, much like the Hibernian Society for the Irish.

The Grecian Society purchased property at St. Philip and Fishburne Streets and built the first Holy Trinity Greek Orthodox Church in Charleston, which was dedicated on March 25, 1911. The lot on which the church was built was purchased for $700, and the church was built for the sum of $6,500. The cornerstone-laying ceremony was held May 25, 1911. The Reverend Ioachim George and the Reverend Arsenios David of Savannah performed the first service at the church. The *Charleston News and Courier* reported, "Impressive services were held" that morning by the Greeks in Charleston in connection with the laying of the cornerstone. Further reported on that date, church services were held at the old Greek church at Calhoun and Coming Streets. The original Greek church at St. Philip and Fishburne Streets no longer exists, having been torn down to make room for I-26. The chancel screen with icons from the original church, however, were sent to a church in Asheville, North Carolina, and are still in existence.

The fiftieth-anniversary program for the church reports the charter members of the original Grecian Society were: Andrew Anastash, Jimmy Anastash, George Billias, John Billias, Peter Creticos, George Abatielos, Michael Abatielos, Nick Ferendinos, Dionysios Ferendinos, K. Kokkinos, Sam Latto, Nick Lempesis, Costas Christodoulopoulos, John Manuel, Anthony Panayiotou, Gregory Panoutsopoulos, Theodore Papadakos, Demetrios Papadakos, John Meletakos, Spero Skiadaresis, Efstratios Stratakos, Kostas Stratakos, D. Siregelas, Anthanasios Tsiropoulos, Louis Williams, William Xanthakos, James Demos, Angelo Panoutsopoulos, Mike Altine and Anastasios Kiriakis.

The first recorded wedding of church members in Charleston was between John M. Rousso of Paleais, Fokas, Greece, age twenty-five, and Helen Yeitrakis of Athens, Greece, age eighteen. They were married at the Coming and Calhoun Streets location by Nikolaos Hadzivasiliou on October 26, 1914. Witnesses to the marriage were Spero Schiadaressi and Michael Pavlou.

In 1914, property was acquired adjacent to the church on St. Philip Street and was used as a meeting place, priest's residence and as a school for teaching the Greek language. In 1923, the priest's residence was remodeled and converted into two classrooms. Here, Sunday school classes were held, and every weekday afternoon, young Greek Americans were taught the language of their parents. By 1938 there was even a kindergarten, with Mr. Paul J. Efstathiou as director.

In the early 1930s, the property adjacent to the church on St. Philip Street proved too small for a community center and parochial school, and a larger building was necessary. Also during the 1930s, the first choir was organized by Alex Tumboli, and he was the first choir director.[19] Prior to that time, the music of the church had been provided solely by the parish priest and by cantors. Margaret Gazes Morris was the first church organist.[20] Subsequently, Tony Hadgi composed musical arrangements for the choir. From 1936 to 1940, Mr. Hadgi was the first conductor of the Charleston Symphony Orchestra.

By 1938, with John G. Fludas as president; P.P. Leventis Sr. as vice-president; Nicholas D. Anthony (Athanasatos) as secretary; Andrew Tumboli as treasurer; and Jerry M. Moskos, John P. Liatos and Peter H. Creticos as directors, a building fund with $4,000 as the initial sum was started for the construction of the Hellenic Community Center on Race Street. The original plans for the Hellenic Community Center called for it to be erected next to the parish house on St. Philip Street, but it was decided that the property at 30 Race Street was more suitable. The Hellenic Center property was

The original Greek Orthodox Church of the Holy Trinity in Charleston, which no longer exists, was located on Coming and St. Philip Streets. Its location is now part of I-26.

Photo taken at the funeral of Frank M. Cockinos in 1923 in front of the original Greek Orthodox church in Charleston. This photograph was provided courtesy of Stuhr's Funeral Home. Note most of the attendees are male, probably because the early Greek immigrants were predominately men who came to America to seek their fortunes and return home. Once in America, however, most all of them stayed. Women later arrived to become their brides.

Kindergarten, circa 1938. *Back row*: Paul J. Efstathiou, Mary Kirlaki Pappas, Reverend Bartholomew Karahalios. *Second row*: Flora Christopoulo Mamakos, Peter Demos Jr., Panos J. Liatos, Chris J. Theos, Stella J. Rousso. *First row*: Pano P. Lamis Jr., Kerry D. Gionis, Sophia Lawandales Demos, Lucia Manos Morfesis, Tula Carosatos Demetre, Spero N. Drake and Nicholas J. Panos.

purchased from the City of Charleston for $5,000. The center was built for the low bid of $27,084.27. Plato Chapter No. 4, Order of AHEPA, assisted by depositing $1,200 in an account for the building fund. Ground was broken for the new Hellenic Community Center on October 28, 1940.

The center was designed by architect Augustus E. Constantine and was dedicated September 28, 1941. Constantine was born in Greece and trained at Georgia Tech. He was a prominent architect of Greek ancestry in Charleston and designed the American Theatre, the Morris Street Baptist Church and the Arcade Theater, among other structures in the city. Constantine considered himself a classicist, as referenced in the *News and Courier*. The Hellenic Center had a classical design as originally constructed, although its façade was changed as a result of later expansion.

The Hellenic Center Building Committee consisted of Reverend B.A. Karahalios and John G. Fludas, general chairman and secretary; John P. Liatos, chairman; Peter P. Leventis Sr., treasurer; Augustus E. Constantine, architect; and George Christopoulo, Demetrios D. Diasourakis, Peter P. Demos, Angelo G. Drakos, Nicholas H. Gianaris, George C. Hitopoulos, Sam M. Latto, Jerry M. Moskos, Jerry Prosalentis, John M. Rousso, Nicholas G. Theos and Athanas T. Tsiropoulos.

The Hellenic Community Center as originally constructed in 1940. The building still exists, although with a new façade due to renovations. The architect for the original building was Augustus E. Constantine.

The 1940 completion of the Hellenic Center. *First row*: Mary Kirlaki Pappas, Nicky Gazes, Mnosto Rosopoulos Stamatiades, Litsa Gregorakis Tumboli, Helen Kaperonis Leventis. *Second row*: Nicholas H. Gianaris, George Hitopoulos, Nicholas G. (Theos) Theodoratos, Sam M. Latto, Reverend Bartholomew Karahalios, John P. Liatos, Nicholas H. Gianaris, Peter P. Demos.

Above left: Peter P. Leventis Sr. served as president of the Parish Council of the Greek Orthodox church in Charleston for many years and was instrumental in the establishment of the church on Race Street.

Above right: Sam M. Latto served as Parish Council president and chairman of the Church Building Committee (1942–52). He was instrumental in the establishment of the church on Race Street.

The dedication ceremonies for the Hellenic Center on Race Street were elaborate. Archbishop Athenagoras, primate of the Greek Orthodox Church of North and South America, officiated; the president of the Parish Council, John G. Fludas, spoke; John P. Liatos was toastmaster; and the Reverend B.A. Karahalios, the priest at the time, introduced the Archbishop. The Greek Schoolteachers at that time were Paul J. Efstathiou, principal, and Mrs. Mary Kirlaki Pappas, teacher. Present at the dedication of the Hellenic Community Center was the first Parish Council president, Theodore Papadakos. An auction was held for the key to the building, which went to Peter P. Leventis Sr. The original Hellenic Community Center consisted of a church office, a small printing room, two classrooms, a meeting room and a kitchen on the first floor. The second floor consisted of the auditorium with stage, dressing room and a refreshment area. From the time the Hellenic Center was dedicated, the Greeks of Charleston concentrated on still another goal; a new and larger church next to the Hellenic Community Center.

All during the Second World War, plans were formulated for the church. Fundraising drives were held, and all of the Greek community organizations, fraternal and religious, combined their efforts to build the new church.

At a General Assembly meeting held on May 16, 1943, a permanent committee was elected to undertake the building of the new church. Original committee members elected were: Sam M. Latto, chairman; Peter P. Demos, treasurer; Peter P. Leventis Sr.; D. Stefanatos; Chris Pepergias; Frank E. Lawandales; John M. Rousso; Valsamakis Magoulas; George T. Savvas; Demetrios K. Manolatos (Manos); Socrates Schiadaressi; and Tom Gianatos.

Between 1946 and 1948, additional members were added and the committee consisted of the following individuals, as listed on a bronze plaque found in the Narthex of the church: Reverend Joachim Malachias, Reverend Modestos Stavrides, Reverend Nicholas C. Trivelas. Executive Committee: Sam M. Latto, chairman; John P. Liatos, vice-chairman; Nicholas G. Theos, secretary; Theodore C. Varras, secretary; Peter P. Demos, treasurer; Peter P. Leventis Sr., financial chairman; and Nick J. Christopoulou, Demetrios G. Diasourakis and Constan J. Moskos, committee members. General Committee: Athanasios G. Anagnostopoulos, Fred Chacharonis, Diasouris D. Diasourakis, Nicholas H. Garbis, Stanley E. Georgeo, Nicholas H. Gianaris, Nick Gianatos, Frank E. Lawandales, John Milton, Jerry M. Moskos, John M. Rousso, George T. Savvas and Athanasios T. Tsiropoulos. Recording Secretaries: Andrew Alissandratos and Gus S. Ballis. Legal advisors: J.D.E. Meyer and Louis Shimel. Architect: Harold Tatum. Builder: Dotterer Engineering Co.

Augustus E. Constantine was further authorized to design the new Greek Orthodox church on Race Street. He completed his design in the late 1940s, again following the classical approach, although the interior of the church was to be of Byzantine design. This is an unusual design, but not without precedent. A church of similar design exists on the Island of Corfu. Archbishop Athenagoras—then Archbishop of North and South America, who was later elevated to the status of Ecumenical Patriarch of Constantinople and became Athenagoras the First in November 1948—suggested to the Building Committee when plans were presented to be approved for the Constantine

Drawing depicting Hellenic Community Center, designed by Augustus E. Constantine, and his proposed plan for the new church, incorporating classic Greek design although with a Byzantine interior. This plan was later abandoned for the Byzantine church that now exists on Race Street.

Groundbreaking on October 8, 1950. *Left to right*: George C. Kanellos, past president; Ted Schedaressi, son of past president; Dr. Peter C. Gazes, son of past president; Mrs. Efterpi Michaels, daughter of past president Kosta M. Kokkinos; Panos J. Liatos, icon bearer; Athanas T. Tsiropoulos, past president; Peter P. Leventis Sr., president.

design that it would be appropriate to give something unique to the city of Charleston, and he suggested a Byzantine structure. It was thus determined at the suggestion of Archbishop Athenagoras that the classical design not be followed and that the church have a Byzantine design.

The groundbreaking was held on October 8, 1950, and the cornerstone for the new Holy Trinity Greek Orthodox Church at 28 Race Street was laid on March 4, 1951. The officers and members of the Parish Council at the time of this historic occasion were: Peter P. Leventis Sr., president; Constan J. Moskos, vice-president; Stanley E. Georgeo, secretary; Demetrios (Jimmy) D. Diasourakis, treasurer; and Theodore C. Varras, Frank H. Panegeris, Harry N. Gianaris, J. Louis Lempesis, Alex J. Tumboli, Angelo J. Demos and Harry C. Trapales as members. Harry N. Gianaris, born February 3, 1927, and Demetrios (Jimmy) D. Diasourakis, born August 7, 1925, were the youngest members on the Parish Council at that time.

On May 17, 1953, the church was dedicated with Archbishop Michael officiating as the newly appointed Archbishop of North and South America after the elevation of Athenagoras as Ecumenical Patriarch of Constantinople. Father Nicholas C. Trivelas performed the first wedding in the new church, marrying Socrates P. Creticos and Zilla Buddin.

Harold Tatum served as the architect in consultation with Archbishop Michael with respect to the design of the church, the iconostasion (chancel screen) and altar. Eugene

Church Building Committee 1952. *Seated*: Father Nicholas C. Trivelas; Theodore C. Varras, secretary; Sam M. Latto, chairman; John P. Liatos, vice-chairman; Peter P. Demos, treasurer; Peter P. Leventis Sr., campaign chairman. *Standing*: Demetrios G. Diasourakis, Charles P. Trapalis Jr., Theodore A. Tsiropoulos, Nicholas G. (Theodoratos) Theos, Nicholas J. Christopoulo, George T. Savvas, Elias S. Latto. *Absent*: Constan J. Moskos, John C. Castanes.

Witnessing the signing of new church contract. *Seated*: Sam M. Latto, chairman of Building Committee; Peter P. Leventis Sr., president of Parish Council; Theodore C. Varras, secretary of Building Committee. *Standing*: Father Nicholas C. Trivelas; E. Gailliard Dotterer, builder; Alex G. Tumboli, trustee; Constan J. Moskos, trustee and member of Building Committee; Gus S. Ballis, recording secretary; John P. Liatos, vice-chairman of Building Committee; Harold D. Tatum, architect.

New church on Race Street dedicated May 17, 1953.

Dotterer of Dotterer Engineering Co. was the builder. The total cost of the church on Race Street, including interior furnishings, exceeded $300,000.

In October 1975, the church became "debt free" when the mortgage was paid in full. The satisfied mortgage was auctioned, with George D. Bazakas being the highest bidder. The mortgage is framed and hangs in the boardroom of the Parish Council.

Byzantine architecture has as its model the Hagia Sophia, the Church of the Holy Wisdom of God, built in the fourth century by Emperor Justinian of the Byzantine empire. It features vaults and arches, domes, patterns in low relief, mosaics and rich, sumptuous colors. The central dome of Holy Trinity rises fifty feet and contains thirteen windows that depict the life of Christ from the Annunciation to the Ascension. There are six chandeliers, four feet in diameter, which are copies of the eighteen-foot-diameter chandeliers in Hagia Sophia. Two of these chandeliers, one in the choir's loft and the other behind the bishop's throne, are from the original church. Three candle stands (manoulia), a wooden dome icon stand and an icon of the Holy Trinity when you enter the church from Race Street are from the original church at St. Philip and Fishburne Streets. The church is divided into the Narthex, where tradition says the learners stand; the Nave, where believers stand; the Solea, where the seven sacraments take place; and the Sanctuary, which represents heaven and is where the Eucharist is kept.

Image of icon screen.

When the Building Committee was looking for an iconographer for the new church, Sam M. Latto remembered having read in a Greek newspaper that Archbishop Michael had presented an icon of the Holy Mother Mary by iconographer Photis Kontoglou to Eva Peron during a pastoral visit in Argentina, and suggested Kontoglou to the Building Committee. It was decided that if the Archbishop had chosen Kontoglou's icon to present to Eva Peron, he must have some importance as a Byzantine iconographer. Accordingly, Kontoglou was contacted and he painted the following:

The Nymphios (Bridegroom) moveable icon; first icon by Kontoglou sent to Charleston to display his work.

Templon icons (Iconostasion), as follows: the Holy Trinity, Archangel Michael, the Blessed Mother Mary and Child, the Lord Jesus Christ, St. John the Baptist, Archangel Gabriel, the Last Supper.

Medallion icons, as follows: Saints Katherine, Nicholas, Constantine and Helen, Demetrios, Annunciation, Transfiguration, Epiphany, Saints Peter and Paul, Gerasimos, George, Andrew and John Chrysostom. Kontoglou sent his collaborator, George N. Gliatas, to Charleston in 1953 to personally deliver and mount these icons. Prior to Gliatas's arrival in Charleston, the medallion icon of Constantine and Helen (located on the western lower dome of the church) was exhibited in Paris, France, and received a citation. The icons are of substantial value due to the importance of Kontoglou as an

St. Gerasimos.

iconographer. Kontoglou wanted the icons to be a testament to his work in America. Kontoglou was honored by the Pope of Rome for his revival of true Christian art and was also recognized by the Archbishiop of Canterbury.

During Gliatas's visit to Charleston, he painted the following icons:

    a) Crucifixion, processional cross and corpus (Efstavromenos)

    b) Holy Mother Mary and Christ Child (Rodon ton Amaranton), moveable icon

    c) Narthex icons: Holy Trinity and the Repose of the Virgin Mary (Koimisis Tis Theotokou)

The Nave stained-glass windows are copies of work of Photis Kontoglou, with the exception of the Annunciation, which was purchased from Lloren Stained Glass Studios.

Father Nicholas C. Trivelas became parish priest on Mother's Day, May 9, 1948, and continued to serve as parish priest until his retirement on August 31, 1993. He thereafter continued to serve the parish in an emeritus status. With Father Nick's interest and inspiration, additional iconography was completed in the church following the Kontoglou designs. In February 1982, John Terzis, an iconographer from Chicago, Illinois, and a collaborator of Kontoglou, painted the area above the Holy Altar, the *Platytera* (the Mother of God and Christ Child) and the *Philoxenia* (the Hospitality of Abraham and Sara).

After the *Platytera* iconography was damaged by Hurricane Hugo in 1989, it was ultimately restored in March 1998 by Emmanouel Tzirtzilakis, another collaborator of Photis Kontoglou. Substantial restoration work was otherwise accomplished in the interior

Left column, top to bottom: St. Katherine, St. Nicholas, Saints Constantine and Helen.
Right column, top to bottom: St. Demetrios, the Annunciation, Saints Peter and Paul.

of the church under the chairmanship of Jimmie A. Gianoukos, with the assistance of Constantine (Dinos) D. Liollio as architect, and was completed in April 1997. Constantine (Dinos) D. Liollio and his father, Demetrios C. Liollio, served the church professionally over many years as prominent architects. Many individuals contributed financially to the restoration project, and the estate of George D. Bazakas, who was a member of the parish and an ardent supporter thereof, provided significant funds in support of this endeavor.

More recently, Emmanouel Tzirtzilakis was commissioned as iconographer and painted the following within the interior of the church:

1. In August 1999, full length-icons on the altar lower wall with the figures St. Gregory the Theologian, St. John Chrysostom, St. Basil the Great and St. Athanasios.

2. In August 2002, "Christ the Pantocrator" together with the "Heavenly Hosts/Angels" on the dome.

3. In July 2003, "The Heavenly Divine Liturgy" on the dome.

4. In May 2005, the Transepts above the Nave doors depicting the "Land of the Living" and "Baby Jesus Reclining." In the altar: Proskomide, "Extreme Humility" (Akra Tapeinosis); Sacristy, "St. John the Baptist."

After construction of the new church, it soon became apparent that the community was outgrowing its facilities and additional classroom space was needed. A Sunday school building committee was formed in 1956 and in 1958 the work of the committee was submitted for approval to the Parish Council and the General Assembly of the community. Approval was granted and Demetrios C. Liollio was named architect for the project. The Building Committee for the Sunday school consisted of Reverend Nicholas C. Trivelas, Chairman Andrew P. Leventis Sr., Gus S. Ballis, Paul J. Gelegotis, Elias S. Latto, Nicolas G. Latto and Demetrios C. Liollio as architect.

The groundbreaking was held Sunday, April 3, 1960, and the cornerstone ceremony was held Sunday, May 22, 1960, with the Right Reverend Germanos officiating. The cornerstone was donated by McCarthy and Sons. The highest bidder for the trowel was Tom A. Fergos.

The dedication of the Sunday school building was held during the Golden Anniversary of Holy Trinity, December 3–4, 1960, with Athenagoras Kavadas of Theiateron, Archbishop of England and Central Europe, officiating. (Archbishop Kavadas was the first schoolmaster and cofounder of Holy Cross Seminary with Patriarch Athenagoras in Brookline, Massachusetts.)

The education building to the rear of the Hellenic Center consists of six classrooms, twenty-two feet by thirty-feet. The construction cost amounted to approximately $67,240. Teachers of the Greek School were Father Nikolaos Hadzivasiliou (1915–16) and Father Vasilios Papaṇikas (1923–24). The first full-time teacher was Hionia N. Christopoulo, who organized the school in 1923. Soon after followed Mrs. Natalia Lazarides (1925–26), Paul J. Efstathiou and Mary Kirlaki Pappas (1931–42) and Theo Theodorou (1942–43).

Additional teachers of the Greek School during the 1940s to the 1980s were John C. Chrysostom (principal), Helen C. Ballis, Gus S. Ballis, Dennis G. Latto (who was later ordained a priest), Irene Loverdou, Irene Ferderigos Fokas, Fred Fotion (graduate of Brookline Theological Seminary), Penelope Gianaris, Eleftheria Papanikolopoulos (graduate of St. Basil's Academy), Alexandra Demos Stefanou, Faye Trivelas Zoeller,

Iconography on the dome of the Greek Orthodox church in Charleston.

Alexandra Franklin, Helen W. Lefter, Eftihia Dimakopoulos Avgeropoulos, Polimia Aliferakis, Nike Araliou Pappas, Nena Horton Chakeris (substitute), Yolanda Tumboli Demos, Voula Sakoglou Aslanidis (assistant), Urania Fokas Nikatos (assistant), Smaragda Nastou Huddleston (adult evening classes) and Koula Papadimitriou Kordonis, who started teaching the upper classes in 1996 and is still teaching as of 2008.

Reverend Nicholas C. Trivelas was appointed by the Parish Council as principal and also served as teacher for nine years. Cleo A. Stoucker has served as teacher from 1978–83, 1990–94 and became director/teacher of the Greek school in 1994. She is still teaching as of 2008.

Greek poems are traditionally recited to mark the independence of Greece from Turkish rule, which was declared on March 25, 1821. These poems have been recited each year by students of the Afternoon School of Modern Greek and herald a love for the motherland and ideals of freedom and liberty. Also marking Greek independence, the mayor of the city of Charleston traditionally signs a proclamation acknowledging this event and the contributions of Greece to democracy.

The education building also provided a nursery that was open five mornings a week. Teachers at the nursery provided Greek language instruction to prepare children for afternoon Greek school and the nursery existed from 1952 through 1978. The preschool teachers serving through this period were Helen Andreou Ballis (1952–53); Irene Loverdou (1959–64); Olga Carras Kirlis, assistant (1961–71); Vasso Korbos Trapalis, assistant (1963–64); Yolanda Tumboli Demos (1971–73); Karen Lempesis Green, substitute (1972–73); Betty Hormovitis Manos, substitute (1972–73); Eleftheria Papanikolopoulos, graduate of St. Basil's Academy (1973–77); and Effie Harzas Stamatiades (1977–78).

In 1959–61, during the tenure of Athena Critikos Gazes as president of the Philoptochos, a church-affiliated organization, the first church library was established with her mother, Katherine Tsigris Critikos, designated as librarian/historian. From 1964 until January 1985, Mary Mamalakis Botzis continued the library.

In the summer of 1991, the library was reorganized by Athena Critikos Gazes and a large staff of volunteers and by the fall, the library was in operation. The library contains circulation and reference areas as well as areas for videos and children's and teen books.

Image of the Sunday school, June 22, 1949. Pictured are Father Nicholas C. Trivelas, Sunday school teachers and students.

Signing of a proclamation for Greek Independence Day, March 25, at the office of Mayor William McG Morrison. *Standing*: Mary Pepergias Castanes, GAPA representative; Paul J. Gelegotis, president of Parish Council; Reverend Nicholas C. Trivelas; Mary Poulos Pavlis, president of Philoptochos Ladies Society; Angelo A. Anastopoulo, AHEPA representative.

All materials are primarily Orthodox- or Christian-related, and there is also reference material on other religions. All titles are donated to the library in honor or in memory of someone or to the glory of God. The library is known as the Reverend Nicholas C. Trivelas Library and Bookstore. It has in excess of 3,000 books and 380 videos and as of December 31, 2005, it had a total value in excess of $64,000.

On a cultural note, the Greeks have always treasured theater, music and poetry. Theatrical and musical productions were staged in Charleston in the Greek language and were played to the Greek community for many years into the 1950s. The mandolin, popular on the island of Cephalonia, from which many of the Greeks in Charleston migrated, is evidenced in a photograph in this book taken in 1934. On that occasion, various "mandolinatatas" were played for a theatrical production entitled *Night of Charity*.

Greek operettas had their origins in the Ionian islands between Italy and Greece and were influenced by Italian opera. Numerous Greek operettas were staged in Charleston, probably because many of the Charleston Greeks came from these islands. The creative hand of Alex Tumboli is noteworthy in many of these productions, which were enthusiastically supported by the Greek community.

1931 theatrical production at Columbus Hall. *Left to right*: (unknown), Dionysios Stefanatos, Helen Kasimatis Palassis, Jerry Magoulas, Margaret Gazes, Xeni Vlassopoulou Drake, George Hitopoulos, Chris Pappas. *Seated*: Andrew A. Trapalis, Julia (Chrysanthe) W. Lempesis.

The Mandolin Players. *Seated*: Paraskevoula C. Pepergias, Julia (Chrysanthe) W. Lempesis, Mary Kirlaki Pappas. *Standing*: Theodore Kypreos, Anna P. Creticos, Margaret Gazes, Nicky Gazes, Demos P. Pappas.

The last Greek operetta staged in Charleston was entitled *Elvira* and was presented by choir members and parishioners at Rivers High School in 1957 under the direction of Professor Luke Pappas, who taught at The Citadel. The accompanists on that occasion were Mary N. Drake and Stella N. Gianatos as assistant. This same operetta sponsored by GOYA was staged for the Golden Anniversary celebration of Holy Trinity Greek Orthodox Church and was again presented at Rivers High School on December 3, 1960.

In 1948, a Charleston Hellenic Choral Group was organized by Mary Economy as organist and led by Eclecte A. Tsiropoulos. This group presented various concerts and raised money for the building of the new church on Race Street.

In 1952, Father Nicholas C. Trivelas had the idea of a Male Chorus, and in June 1953, he issued an invitation to young males to join the chorus to learn "both religious and secular pieces, to sing at special services and to present choral concerts."

The original members of the chorus were Ernest A. Babanats, Tony P. Chrisanthis, Peter Demos Jr., Spero N. Drake, George P. Gigis, Kerry D. Gionis, Pano P. Lamis, Elias

First performance of the a capella Male Chorus. *First row*: Reverend Nicholas C. Trivelas, Protopresbyter; Costan D. Pappas; Demetre J. Liatos; Peter Demos Jr.; His Grace Germanos Polizoides, Bishop of Nyssa; Spero N. Drake; George P. Gigis; Ross A. Magoulas. *Second row*: Costan A. Magoulas; Stellios F. Lawandales; Nicholas J. Theos; Stathy A. Tumboli; Pano P. Lamis Jr.; Kerry D. Gionis. *Third row*: Tony P. Chrisanthis; George Barber; John P. Stamatiades; Anthony J. Tellis; Marcos D. Stratos. *Fourth row*: George P. Saclarides; John W. Perry; Theodore T. Savvas; Elias S. Latto; Thymie (Tim) S. Latto.

S. Latto, Thymie (Tim) S. Latto, Eleas F. Lawandales, Stellios F. Lawandales, Demetre J. Liatos, Panos J. Liatos, Constan A. Magoulas, Ross A. Magoulas, Costan D. Pappas, George P. Saclarides, Theodore T. Savvas, Anthony (Tony) J. Tellis, Nick J. Theos, Chris J. Theos, Pete J. Theos, Stathy A. Tumboli and John W. Perry.

The Male Chorus trained by Father Nicholas C. Trivelas sang four-part music for male voices written by Speros Bekatoros. This music was sung by the Greek Orthodox Seminary of the Holy Cross, Pomfret Center, Connecticut. The Male Chorus made its first appearance at the Arahovitiko Festival in Gastonia, North Carolina, in 1953, singing the Archierarchal Divine Liturgy.

Since its inception, the Male Chorus has sung the Divine Liturgy at Holy Trinity Greek Orthodox Church and for numerous wedding services in Charleston, and in neighboring Greek Orthodox parishes. Additionally, during the years 1987–90 and in 1993, the Male Chorus participated in the "Festival of Churches" during the Piccolo Spoleto Festival in Charleston. Programs were presented to the public during Spoleto consisting of hymns in four-part harmony. In addition, several hymns were chanted in the monophonic Byzantine tradition using a drone note (ISON).

In addition to the Charleston Hellenic Choral Group (which no longer exists) and the Male Chorus, there have been various church choirs that sing the Divine Liturgy during church services, including a Junior Choir organized by Father Trivelas in 1952 and taught by Ross A. Magoulas, a mixed choir and a Women's Choir. The Women's Choir was begun when Ross A. Magoulas and Mary Drake Perry, both avidly interested in church liturgical music, contacted Anna Gallos about composing the Liturgy with arrangements explicitly for women's voices. With this accomplished, the Women's Choir was organized and the original members were Anna Nikolaou Chrysostom, Jane Ann R. Deaton, Christina P. Demos, Hope Gazes Grayson, Toula S. Latto, Diane Stamas Mashead, Katina Corontzes Manos, Mary Gigis Moskos, Mary R. Palassis, Dena J. Panos, Aphrodite (Aphro) Stevens Pappas, Presvytera Elena Gavrilis Savas, Lucy Stupenos Spell, Cali-Ann Rodes Spyropoulos, Katherine Gigis Theos, Frances (Froso) C. Trapales and Mary Gelegotis Zervos, with Mary Drake Perry as organist and Ross A. Magoulas as director.

The music of the church in Charleston originally was sung only in the Greek language, but over the years it has been sung in both Greek and in English. During the tenure of Father Nicholas C. Trivelas, he taught the hymns of the Liturgy in Greek to all Sunday school students during the children's worship service (Paidiki Akolouthia). From the early 1970s until 1993, the Junior Choir of the church—redesignated the Sunday School Choir—began singing the entire Liturgy in Greek under the direction of Rosa P. Paulatos, Faye Trivelas Zoeller and Hope Gazes Grayson, assisted by Cathy P. Gazes. Beginning in 1997, the Sunday School Choir began singing the Liturgy in English and only certain hymns in Greek under the direction of Mary Drake Perry, Cali-Ann Rodes Spyropoulos and Penelope C. Jebeles. In later years, the Women's Choir and Mixed Choir began singing the entire Liturgy in either Greek, English or both at various church services.

The Charleston Bouzoukia[21] was organized around 1962, providing not only entertainment that raised funds for the Greek community, but also popularizing Greek song and dance within the Charleston community at large. Arthur (Art) S. Homer

Church choir, circa 1938. Seated to the left of the priest, Reverend George Nicolaides, is Margaret Gazes Morris, the first organist for the church. To the right is Mary Kirlaki Pappas, who taught at the afternoon church school for many years.

Choir photo taken in interior of the original Greek Orthodox church in Charleston, South Carolina. *First row*: Chanter Kyriakos Smyrniotis, (unknown), Mary Gigis Moskos, Rosie Leventis Billas, Lula Gigis Latto, Betty Lamis Lawandales, Alice Tellis Critikos, Mary Rose Palassis, Katherine Gigis Theos, Mary Pappas Lawandales, Reverend Nicholas C. Trivelas. *Second row*: Christine Savvas Homer, Frances (Froso) C. Trapales, Stella Moskos Tshontikides, Kiki Misoyianis Billias, Vera J. Tellis, Joan Carabatsos Magoulas, Georgia Leventis Kampakis, Margaret N. Klonaris, Dia G. Misoyianis. *Third row*: Peter Demos Jr., Ross A. Magoulas, Ernest A. Babanats, Harry G. Speliopoulos Spell, Thymie (Tim) S. Latto, Nicholas N. Klonaris, Panos J. Liatos, Nicholas J. Theos.

Women's Choir. *First row*: Mary Drake Perry (organist), Hope Gazes Grayson, Mary Gigis Moskos, Jane Ann R. Deaton, Mary Rose Palassis, Katherine Gigis Theos, Katina Corontzes Manos, Presvytera Elena Gavrilis Savas. *Second row*: Ross A. Magoulas (director), Cali-Ann Rodes Spyropoulos, Aphrodite (Aphro) Stevens Pappas, Anna Nikolaou Chrysostom, Diane Stamas Mashead, Mary Gelegotis Zervos, Lucy Stupenos Spell, Dena J. Panos, Christina P. Demos, Toula S. Latto. *Not pictured*: Frances (Froso) C. Trapales.

acted as band leader and Tony Hadgi, who was with the Charleston Symphony Orchestra, provided musical direction and arrangements for the group. The group played not only in Charleston but in a majority of major cities in the South as well, including Jacksonville, Charlotte, Columbia, Augusta, Atlanta and Wilmington. More recently, in the 1970s, Nick N. Trivelas, the son of Father Nicholas C. Trivelas, organized a bouzoukia band known as The Aegeans, which played not only in Charleston but around the nation. George C. Fassuliotis, John G. Misoyianis and other players who performed in the Charleston Bouzoukia have provided music for the benefit of the church in Charleston with respect to its festivals and other events.

In March 1960, numbers 15 and 17 Race Street, which were located across the street from the church, were purchased for $11,500. In 1962, the church purchased 19 Race Street for the sum of $19,000. These three lots across the street from the church are used for church parking.

In September 1976, the church, with George J. Morris as president, purchased the Mayflower Court, consisting of fourteen rental units adjacent to the church, for $100,000, with financing provided by the owner J.C. Long through a low-interest loan.

On July 1, 1980, the Hellenic Center was vacated. It was renovated after many years of discussion at a total cost of $467,913.21. The work was done by Wieters Construction Company and Demetrios C. Liollio was the architect. The keys to the newly renovated

Bouzoukia band. *First row*: Savas J. Canacaris, Emanuel S. Redman, George C. Fassuliotis, Ernest (Taso) G. Misoyianis, Ernest Horres. *Second row*: John G. Misoyianis, Eleftherios (Al) E. Kirlis. *Third row*: John G. Kanellos, Diane Stamas Mashead, Frances (Froso) C. Trapales, Arthur (Art) S. Homer. *Not pictured*: John P. Manos, Athanasios (Tom) Vlismas, Constantinos (Deno) G. Servis, Tony Hadgi.

Hellenic Center were turned over to the renovation chairman, Harry G. Hitopoulos, on August 14, 1981.

A donation received by the church from the estates of Peter and Harry Chrisantou was instrumental in the renovation of the Hellenic Center. This donation, approximately $100,000, was put toward the renovation. The General Assembly voted March 18, 1984, to dedicate the auditorium of the renovated Hellenic Center as Chrisantou Hall.

In July 1988, the parish purchased property adjacent to the Hellenic Center, known as the Hogan House, and the cottage to the rear thereof for a total cost of $65,000. The owner, Camille B. Hogan, had obtained the property in 1928, when it was one of the original structures on Race Street. The main residence was built in 1912 by Camille Hogan's father, and has historic significance, details of which are set forth in a *News and Courier* article entitled "Resident Recalls Race St.'s Rural Roots In Last Century," published Monday, October 25, 1982.

More recently, the fourteen rental units on the Mayflower Court property were removed and relocated to the rear of the Darlington Apartments on King Street Extension with governmental funds provided to remove and renovate these properties for low-income housing. The Mayflower Court property was then landscaped to become a park that has been used in conjunction with festivals held by the Greek community on an annual basis and for parking. In 2007, an icon of the Virgin Mary was erected in the park and the adjacent area was set aside to serve as a place of prayer and reflection. The area is named the Garden of the Theotokos. His Eminence Metropolitan Alexios, spiritual leader of the Greek Orthodox Church in the Southeast, dedicated the Icon of the Virgin Mary on April 12, 2008.

Greeks have always been proud of their heritage, cuisine and hospitality. As a consequence, not only in Charleston, but in other Greek communities around the nation, Greek festivals sponsored by the Greek Orthodox church of the local community are regularly held, with an emphasis on Greek food, music, culture and the Orthodox faith. Charleston is no exception, and its festivals have been held for many years at Middleton Gardens, Charles Towne Landing, Francis Marion Square and, more recently, on the grounds of the Holy Trinity Greek Orthodox Church. The people who have given their time and talent to make these festivals possible are too numerous to mention. These events have been successful in promoting the Greek community and have raised funds for the benefit of the church and its good works and in the process have provided camaraderie to the participants and substantial enjoyment to those who attend.

In the 1970s, the church grounds began to be the site of a traditional "Easter Glendi." At first the Glendi was held at the rear of the Hellenic Center and more recently on the Mayflower Court property. Traditionally, after midnight Easter Resurrection services, families would gather to break the Lenten fast with lamb, a traditional Greek sweet bread and Easter eggs all dyed red, symbolizing the blood of Christ. As this practice declined in family homes, it was determined to have the traditional Easter Glendi on the church grounds after the Easter Sunday Agape service, when the Good News of the New Testament is spread by the reading of the Gospel in numerous languages. This Glendi has become very successful, with parishioners and their acquaintances participating in this joyous occasion that is steeped in Greek tradition.

In 2004, the Strategic Planning Committee of the church, headed by Jimmie A. Gianoukos, presented an application for the Holy Trinity Church to be placed on the National Historic Register. The nomination as presented was approved by the State of South Carolina Historic Preservation Office, thereby listing the church at the state level of historic places. Efforts are still underway to have the church placed on the national level. Furthermore, the church, on recommendation of Constantine (Dinos) D. Liollio, has voluntarily placed itself under the jurisdiction of the Charleston Board of Architectural Review so as to best protect the unique Byzantine character of the church and its surrounding properties.

In 2005, the church purchased property at 11 Race Street, substantially below market value, from Plato Chapter No. 4, Order of AHEPA, which can be used to provide additional parking for the benefit of the parish. In addition, the historic structure thereon has been renovated for the benefit of the parish. In turn, the Order of AHEPA will make use of the funds obtained therefrom to provide senior citizens with low-income housing for the benefit of the Charleston community.[22]

Greek Food Fair picture. *Left to right*: Lynette (Cissy) Dandridge Morris, Voula Sakoglou Aslanidis, Sandra Croffead Veronee, Gloria Korba Geiger.

Greek Festival dancers in costume. *Left to right*: Nick N. Trivelas on bouzouki, Athan S. Fokas, Daphne P. Vagenas and John P. Manos (dancers).

Photograph of senior citizens following church services, believed to be taken in the 1970s. *First row*: Nicholas A. Pappas, Athanas T. Tsiropoulos. *Second row*: Father Nicholas C. Trivelas, Irene Chronis Pappas, Fotini Armeo Panegeris, Panagiota Alexopoulou Demos, Demetra Mavrantzakis Lawandales, Mahi Galiatsatou Theos, Diane Laskari Billias, George M. Billias. *Third row*: Antonia Palassis Magoulas, John C. Marcotsis, Evanthia Arahovitis Manos, Anthony Maistrellis, (unknown), Pat C. Gazes.

AHEPA house.

Future plans call for the creation of a new Hellenic Center to the rear of the church property to replace the present usage of the Hellenic Center, with the current center either renovated or replaced and with the education building to be incorporated in a new design or replaced as may be appropriate.

PARISH RELATIONSHIP TO ARCHDIOCESE OF THE GREEK ORTHODOX CHURCH OF AMERICA

Holy Trinity Greek Orthodox Church in Charleston is under the jurisdiction of the Archdiocese of the Greek Orthodox Church of America. Holy Trinity was founded in 1910, prior to creation of the Archdiocese, which was formed in 1922 with Archbishop Alexander serving until 1930 as the first Archbishop in America. Subsequent Archbishops were Athenagoras from 1931 to 1948, Michael from 1949 to 1958, Iakovos from 1959 to 1996, Spyridon from 1996 to 1999 and Demetrios from 1999 to the present.

Archbishops do not often visit Charleston. There is no record of Archbishop Alexander having done so. Archbishop Athenagoras, however, did visit the city, and it is noteworthy that he was present at the dedication of the Hellenic Center on Race Street in 1940. Archbishop Michael came for the dedication of the church on Race Street in 1953.

During Archbishop Iakovos's long tenure, he is noted to have visited on two occasions. On one occasion, in addition to his ecclesiastical duties, he also spoke at a meeting of the

Sunday school (June 1940) with his Holiness Ecumenical Patriarch Athenagoras I, serving then as Archbishop of North and South America, and Reverend Bartholomew Karahalios to his right.

Archbishop Michael was in Charleston for the dedication of the church. *Left to right*: John Janis; O.T. Wallace, South Carolina state representative; Peter P. Leventis Sr., president of the Parish Council; Theodore C. Varras, secretary of the Parish Council; Reverend Neophytos Spyridakis, deacon; the Most Reverend Michael, Archbishop North and South America; Reverend Nicholas C. Trivelas, priest, Holy Trinity Greek Orthodox Church, Charleston, South Carolina; Nicholas G. Theos, member of Building Committee; and Sam M. Latto, chairman of Building Committee.

Charleston Chamber of Commerce held at the Francis Marion Hotel. In 1984, he visited for several days on the twenty-fifth anniversary of his ordination as Archbishop. On this visit, Archbishop Iakovos received an honorary degree from the Medical University of South Carolina, presented by Dr. James B. Edwards, the president, who was former governor of the state. He was also honored at a parade at The Citadel and a grand banquet was held with many dignitaries in attendance, including Mayor Joseph P. Riley Jr.; General James W. Duckette, president of The Citadel; Bishop C. FitzSimons Allison of the Episcopal Church; and Bishop Ernest L. Unterkoefler of the Catholic Church. The visit was extensively covered in the *News and Courier*. Many receptions were held in honor of the Archbishop. He was a prominent leader of the church and received the Congressional Medal of Freedom as a champion of civil rights, presented to him by President Jimmy Carter.

Archbishop Spyridon visited Charleston during his tenure and also received an honorary degree from the Medical University.

Catholic Bishop Ernest Unterkoefler greeting Greek Orthodox Archbishop Iakovos during Archbishop Iakovos's visit to the Catholic Cathedral on Broad Street in November 1984.

Major General James A. Grimsley with Archbishop Iakovos at The Citadel dress parade on November 9, 1984, waiting for cadets to pass in review. Pictured on the left of General Grimsley is General Lyman L. Lemnitzer.

EARLY PARISH COUNCIL MINUTES

Through the efforts of Father Nicholas C. Trivelas, Margaret Gazes Morris and Nicky Gazes Pappas, some of the early minutes of the church were translated from Greek to English. They are excerpted as follows:

Earliest Church Minutes:
1914 FIRST MINUTES OF THIS BOOK—5th of Feb. 1914, 46 members in good standing comprised a quorum. Meeting was held in the Greek Church of the Holy Trinity by the General Assembly Chairman Panosologiotatos Nikolaos Hadzivasiliou, with Agiasmos (a blessing of water).

FINANCIAL REPORT was given for year 1913 and including Jan. 1914. Total income was $1,860.13, total expenses was $1387.60 leaving a balance of $472.53.

ELECTION COMMITTEE—President of committee or Chairman Panosologiotatos Nikolaos Hadzivasiliou, Vice Pres. Antonios Panagiotou, Sec'y of committee Konstantinos (Costa Cockinos) Kokkinou.

Elections were conducted for a new Parish Council—

President	Speros Schiaderesis received 34 votes
Vice-President	Gregorios Pansopoulos 34 votes
Secretary	Antonios Panagiotou 31 votes
Treasurer	Konstantinos Christopoulos 35 votes
Council Members	A. Tsiropoulos 38 votes, Vasilios Xanthakis 37 votes, John Meletakos 30 votes, Konstantinos Kokkinos 29 votes—

Runners up:
T. Papadakos, Pres. 9 votes; George Billias Vice Pres. 5 votes; Gregorios Tsiropoulos Treas. 6 votes; Sec K. Kokkinos, 10 votes; Andrew Tumboli 23 votes; Nicholas Lempesis 8 votes.

Theodore Papadakos was cited following elections as past President and it mentions he worked for the establishment of the Grecian Society and he also worked hard for the building of the new Church of the Holy Trinity.

Following that, an auditing committee was elected with Antonios Panagiotou, Konstantinos (Costa Cockinos) Kokkinos, Diasouris Diasourakis, and Nikolaos Lempesis. These men were to check the books from the past Pres. Mr. T. Papadakos.

These minutes were signed by the Election Committee:
President Panosologiolatos Nikolaos Hadzivasiliou, Vice-Pres. A. Panagiotou, no signature by secretary.

This report or minutes of election committee.

Page 5 General Assembly

The association of Charleston Greeks met the 26th of Feb. at 3:00 pm Friday. The 41 members which comprised a quorum met in the local Irish Volunteer Hall. The meeting was called together by the past Pres. and Sec'y and prior to the work of the meeting, Mr. D. Diasourakis read a speech in which he encouraged cooperation and full work for the church and for the school pointing out that every misunderstanding that involved the community and especially the church and the school should be curtailed.

Next a letter was read from the Panhellenic Enosis in which they raised the contributions to the church and school from $100 to $200 a year and also asking for a definite communication between the council with the Panhellenic Enosis.

Financial report was given throughout the year 1914–Jan. 1915, $3,413.79 was collected, $2,704.50 was spent, leaving bal. of $619.29.

Members of election committee elected were—D. Diasourakis, P. Creticos, G. Pansopoulos and G. Manos and they brought forth thru D. Diasourakis the following results of the elections. The following men were elected—Pres. Speros P. Schiaderesis 33 votes; Vice Pres. P. Creticos 11 votes; Treas. K. Christopoulos 18 votes; Secretary D. Diasourakis, 26 votes.

Parish Council members—A. Tsiropoulos 12 votes; Triantafyllos Palassis 15 votes; X.H. Tsiropoulos 19 votes; S. Stratacos 12 votes.

The following slate runners up are as follows; Pres. Pete Creticos 6 votes; Vice Pres. A. Panagiotou 9 votes; Treas. A. Panagiotou 14 votes and Sec'y A. Panagiotou 10 votes and Council members were Antonios Kyriakis 10 votes and A. Panasopoulos 9 votes.

Four member auditing committee was elected—A. Panasopoulos, X.H. Tsiropoulos, K. Moschovakis along with P. Creticos.

The meeting was closed with signatures D. Diasourakis as Eforetiki Epitrope, also signature of Panagiotis Haralambos Creticos.

Minutes No. 56 page 10 Meeting 25 June 1917

Letter of resignation submitted to the board that the priest was resigning. He had problems in Greece. Letter was to be sent to Aidesimotaton Father Ioachim George (Tziotzis) in Pensacola Fla., asking if he would accept the position and under what terms.

Signed by Vice Pres. Schediaressis, Sec. Dd. Diasourkis, council members—A. Aktrab, Nikolaos last name unavailable, John Xanthankos and two other names, not legible.

Minutes No. 56 page 11, Meeting Tues. 8 Aug. 1917

At this meeting it was decided to accept the application of Aidesimotaton Father B.G. Abramopoulos who was serving in Norfolk, Va. sent him a letter to come and serve on Sun. 19 of July and there they could talk in detail.

Mr. Schediaressis Pres., Mr. D. Diasourakis Secy, and Council members A. Panagiotou, A. Arputach, N. Ferentinos, K. Zikos, J. Xanthakos, D. Manos, N. Stratakos.

Minutes No. 57 Page 12 General Assembly Meeting Thurs. Aug. 30, 1917

Meeting held at the Irish Volunteer Hall. D. Diasourakis gave report for the Parish Council for the last 7 months, reporting that $1,811.61 was received and $577.97 spent, leaving balance of $1,233.64.

Auditing Comm. was elected with Gregorios Panasopoulos, Kyriakos Moschovakis and Christos Tsiropoulos.

The resignation of Father Nikolaos Hadgivasiliou was read again and accepted again by the Parish Council and the new letter of the new priest who previously had served here, accepting the application in our community, Aidesimotaton Ioachim George (Tziotzis). Father Ioachim was accepted again.

Members present were—A. Panagiotou, Michael D. Manos, Kyriakos Moschovakis, John Rousso, Gregorios Pansopoulos, D. Demetropoulos, Miltiades D. Logothetis, Athanasios Papalexandrou Papageorgiou, K.E. Christodoulou, Panagiotou X. Creticos, D. Manos, Christos Papachristou, E. Angelopoulos, Alexios Prostatakos, Filippos Voutsas, D. Diasourakis, S. Schediaressis.

Minutes No. 58 pg. 14 11 Oct. 1917

Meeting held in room of S. Schediaressis, letter from Priest Ioachim George (Tziotzis) at which time he accepts the invitation of Parish Council to come and serve in Charleston.

Minutes No. 58 Thurs Oct. 11, 1917

The council met, the letter of Father Ioachim George (Tziotzis) was read and they accepted his coming to Charleston to be their Priest and set his salary as $80.00 a month. In the event that the association would buy a building to house the Priest and also a Greek school, then his salary would be $70.00 a month and living in the house would be part of his salary.

Pres. Schediaressis, Secy D. Diasourakis, Parish Council members N. Stratacos, A. Panagiotou, J. Anastash, Constantinos Zikos, Demetrios Manos, A. Anantios, Ioannis Athos.

Also at this meeting, it was decided for the board of directors to look into buying a building to house the Priest and Greek School.

Minutes No. 59 Tues. 30 Oct. 1917

Purpose of meeting was for the building which was found next to the church, 270 St. Philip St. to be purchased. It was decided unanimously to proceed with this, and a committee was formed with S. Schiaderessi, Konstantinos Christopoulous, A. Panagiotou and Nick Ferentinos to work out details and present this for approval at the following meeting on Tues.

Meeting ended. Present was S. Schiaderessis, Sec'y D. Diasourakis.

Members present—Nicholas Ferentinos, Nicholas Stratacos, A. Panagiotou, Konstantinou Dolou and A. Anastash.

PARISH PRIESTS OF THE GREEK ORTHODOX CHURCH OF THE HOLY TRINITY

1910–1911	Ioachim George (Tziotzis)
January 1914–August 1917	Nikolaos Hadzivasiliou
September 1917	Elias Pavlou (interim priest)
October 17, 1917–January 14, 1919	Ioachim George (Tziotzis)
January 1, 1919–October 1919	Ioannidou
November 1919–February 1921	Vasilios Papanikas
February 18, 1921–April 21, 1921	Vasilios Avramopoulos
April 1921–1922	Nikolaos Hadzivasiliou
1923–1924	Vasilios Papanikas
1926–1929	Pano Stamos
June 1928	Nicholas Papavasiliou (interim priest)
May 1930–1932	Paraskevas Papatheophrastou
1932–September 3, 1933	Meletis Chronides
September 24, 1933–January 1936[23]	Dionysios Papadatos
October 24, 1937–October 9, 1938	George Nicolaides
December 1938–August 1942	Bartholomew Karahalios
November 1942–April 1945	Joachim Malachias
May 1945	Efstathios Spyropoulos (interim priest)
May 1945–May 1, 1948	Modestos Stavrides (Priest Emeritus, 1955–74)
May 9, 1948–August 31, 1993	Nicholas C. Trivelas

Reverend Nicholas C. Trivelas, who came as a new priest in Charleston, arriving Mother's Day, May 9, 1948.

September 1, 1993–July 31, 1996	George P. Savas
August 11, 1996–January 8, 2002	George Tsahakis
January 9, 2002–February 28, 2002	Nicholas C. Trivelas (Priest Emeritus, interim priest)
March 1, 2002–April 30, 2006	John G. Panagiotou
May 1, 2006–July 14, 2006	Nicholas C. Trivelas (Priest Emeritus, interim priest)
July 15, 2006–present	John L. Johns

PARISH COUNCIL OFFICERS AND COUNCIL MEMBERS

Listed below are the officers of the Greek Orthodox Church of the Holy Trinity, Charleston, South Carolina, from 1910 to 1947, as well as past officers and members of the Parish Council of the church from 1949 to 2008.

1910–1913	1914
Theodore Papadakos, **president**	Speros Schiadaressis,[24] **president**
George M. Billias, **vice-president**	Gregory Panoutsopoulos, **vice-president**
John Billias, **secretary**	Anthony Panayiotou, **secretary**
Costas Christodoulopoulos, **treasurer**	Costas Christodoulopoulos, **treasurer**

1915–1917	1918
Speros Schiadaressis, **president**	Anthony Panayiotou, **president**
Peter H. Creticos, **vice-president**	Peter H.Creticos, **vice-president**
D.D. Diasourakis, **secretary**	K. Zekos, **secretary**
	M. Logothetis, **secretary**
Costas Christodoulopoulos, **treasurer**	Nick Ferendinos, **treasurer**

1919	1920
Athanas T. Tsiropoulos, **president**	Athanas T. Tsiropoulos, **president**
William Xanthakos, **vice-president**	Kosta M. Kokkinos, **vice-president**
E. Angelopoulos, **vice-president**	
Isidore C. Psaras, **secretary**	D.D. Diasourakis, **secretary**
Panayiotis Chronis, **secretary**	
Nick Ferendinos, **treasurer**	Nick Ferendinos, **treasurer**

1921	1922
Speros Schiadaressis, **president**	Kosta M. Kokkinos, **president**
George Saclarides, **vice-president**	Costas Christodoulopoulos, **vice-president**
Michael Logothetis, **secretary**	John G. Fludas, **secretary**
Nick Ferendinos, **treasurer**	John C. Palassis, **treasurer**

1923	1924
Costas Christodoulopoulos, **president**	Costas Christodoulopoulos, **president**
Nicholas G. Theodoratos (Theos), **vice-president**	Elias Hadgis, **vice-president**
Nick D. Athanasatos, **secretary**	Nick D. Athanasatos (Anthony), **secretary**
Andrew G. Tumboli, **treasurer**	Andrew G. Tumboli, **treasurer**

1925	1926
Costas Christodoulopoulos, **president**	Costas Christodoulopoulos, **president**
Peter H.Creticos, **vice-president**	Elias Hadgis, **vice-president**
Nick D. Athanasatos (Anthony), **secretary**	D.D. Diasourakis, **secretary**
Nick H. Gianaris, **treasurer**	George M. Latto, **treasurer**

1927	1928
Elias Hadgis, **president**	D.D. Diasourakis, **president**
George C. Kanellos, **vice-president**	George C. Kanellos, **vice-president**
D.D. Diasourakis, **secretary**	John G. Fludas, **secretary**
	E. Markides, **secretary**
George M. Latto, **treasurer**	Sam M. Latto, **treasurer**

1929	1930
Chris D. Gazes, **president**	Chris D. Gazes, **president**
Stylianos Yeitrakis (Sam Trakas), **vice-president**	Stylianos Yeitrakis (Sam Trakas), **vice-president**
	William J. Anagnos, **secretary**
Jerry P. Theodoratos (Theos), **treasurer**	Nick H. Gianaris, **treasurer**

1931	1932
Costas Christodoulopoulos, **president**	John G. Fludas, **president**

George C. Kanellos, **vice-president**	Peter H. Creticos, **vice-president**
Panayiotis Chronis, **secretary**	Evangelos Logothetis, **secretary**
George Hitopoulos, **treasurer**	Jerry M. Moskos, **treasurer**

1933	1934
John G. Fludas, **president**	George C. Kanellos, **president**
William J. Logothetis, **vice-president**	Chris Pappas, **vice-president**
Evangelos Logothetis, **secretary**	Theodore C. Varras, **secretary**
Jerry M. Moskos, **treasurer**	George C. Manos, **treasurer**[25]

1935	1935
William J. Logothetis, **president**	Stylianos Yeitrakis (Trakas), **president**
George Misoyianis, **vice-president**	Peter P. Demos, **vice-president**
Theodore C. Varras, **secretary**	D. Stefanatos, **secretary**
George C. Manos, **treasurer**	George C. Manos, **treasurer**

1936	1937–1938
Demetrius K. Gionis, **president**	John G. Fludas, **president**
Chris Papaioannou, **vice-president**	Peter P. Leventis Sr., **vice-president**
D. Stefanatos, **secretary**	Nick D. Athanastos (Anthony), **secretary**
Theodore Kypraeos, **treasurer**	Andrew G. Tumboli, **treasurer**

1938–1939	1940–1941
John G. Fludas, **president**	John G. Fludas, **president**
Nicholas H. Garbis, **vice-president**	Theodore H. Gianaris, **vice-president**
	Peter H. Creticos, **vice-president**
Nick D. Athanasatos (Anthony), **secretary**	Nick D. Athanasatos (Anthony), **secretary**
Peter P. Leventis Sr., **treasurer**	Peter P. Leventis Sr., **treasurer**

1942–1943	1944–1945
Sam M. Latto, **president**	Sam M. Latto, **president**
John P. Liatos, **vice-president**	John P. Liatos, **vice-president**
Vasilios Kyriakopoulos, **secretary**	Angelo Logothetis, **secretary**
Nicholas G. Theodoratos (Theos), **secretary**	
William Perry, **treasurer**	Augustus E. Constantine, **treasurer**

1937–38 Parish Council. John G. Fludas, president; Peter P. Leventis Sr., vice-president; Nicholas D. Anthony, secretary; Andrew G. Tumboli, treasurer; John P. Liatos, also pictured in center second row. John G. Fludas served as Parish Council president for the years leading up to the groundbreaking for the Hellenic Center on October 28, 1940. The dedication for the Hellenic Center at 30 Race Street was held September 28, 1941, a milestone for the Greek community.

1946–1947
Athanasios T. Tsiropoulos, **president**
John T. Chakeris, **vice-president**
John M. Rousso, **treasurer**
Stylianos Yeitrakis (Sam Trakas), **treasurer**
Nicholas H. Garbis, **secretary**

1948	
president	Peter P. Leventis Sr.
vice-president	Theodore C. Varras
secretary	Andrew Alissandratos
treasurer	Constan J. Moskos

council members	Fred Chacharonis, Demetrios G. Diasourakis, Stanley E. Georgeo, Harry N. Gianaris, Athanasios Kerhoulas, John P. Liatos, William Perry

1949	
president	Peter P. Leventis Sr.
vice-president	Theodore C. Varras
secretary	Theodore C. Varras
treasurer	Constan J. Moskos
council members	Fred Chacharonis, Demetrios G. Diasourakis, Stanley E. Georgeo, Harry N. Gianaris, John P. Liatos, Paul W. Lingos, Ernest (Taso) G. Misoyianis, William Perry

1950	
president	Peter P. Leventis Sr.
vice-president	Theodore C. Varras
secretary	Stanley E. Georgeo
treasurer	Demetrios G. Diasourakis
council members	Angelo J. Demos, Harry N. Gianaris, John G. Kanellos, James C. Manos, Constan J. Moskos, George T. Savvas, Nicholas G. Theos

1951	
president	Peter P. Leventis Sr.
vice-president	Constan J. Moskos
secretary	Stanley E. Georgeo
treasurer	Demetrios G. Diasourakis
council members	Angelo J. Demos, Harry N. Gianaris, J. Louis W. Lempesis, Frank H. Panegeris, Harry C. Trapales, Alex G. Tumboli, Theodore C. Varras

1952	
president	Peter P. Leventis Sr.
vice-president	Stanley E. Georgeo
secretary	Alex G. Tumboli
treasurer	Harry N. Gianaris

council members	Demetrios G. Diasourakis, J. Louis W. Lempesis, James P. Leventis, Frank H. Panegeris, George A. Telegas, Harry C. Trapales, Athanasios (Tom) Vlismas

1953	
president	Peter P. Leventis Sr.
vice-president	Stanley E. Georgeo
secretary	Alex G. Tumboli
treasurer	Harry N. Gianaris
council members	Ernest A. Babanats, George J. Carabatsos, Demetrios G. Diasourakis, James P. Leventis, Frank H. Panegeris, George A. Telegas, Harry C. Trapales

1954	
president	Andrew P. Leventis
vice-president	Nicolas G. Latto
secretary	George P. Saclarides
treasurer	Marko J. Moskos
council members	Mitchell S. Dimitri, Anthony J. Gianoukos, Elias S. Latto, J. Louis W. Lempesis, Peter P. Leventis Sr. (advisor), Constan J. Moskos, Frank H. Panegeris, Anthony N. Pappas

1955	
president	Andrew P. Leventis
vice-president	Nicolas G. Latto
secretary	Elias S. Latto
treasurer	Marko J. Moskos
council members	Gus S. Ballis, Mitchell S. Dimitri, J. Louis W. Lempesis, John G. Misoyianis, Constan J. Moskos, John G. Speliopoulos, George A. Telegas

1956	
president	Gus S. Ballis
vice-president	John G. Speliopoulos
secretary	Elias S. Latto

treasurer	George A. Telegas
council members	Pete E. Banis, William P. Chrisanthis, Harry P. Demos, Pat C. Gazes, Constan A. Magoulas, John G. Misoyianis, Constan J. Moskos

1957	
president	Elias S. Latto
vice-president	Pete E. Banis
secretary	William P. Chrisanthis
treasurer	George A. Telegas
council members	Harry P. Demos, Pat C. Gazes, Paul J. Gelegotis, Constan A. Magoulas, John B. Marcus, John G. Speliopoulos, Harry C. Trapales

1958	
president	Elias S. Latto
vice-president	John G. Speliopoulos
secretary	Paul J. Gelegotis
treasurer	George A. Telegas
council members	Augustine C. Chrysostom, Harry P. Demos, Andrew F. Lawandales, John B. Marcus, Milton D. Stratos, Gregory O. Theos, Harry C. Trapales

1959	
president	Paul J. Gelegotis[26]
vice-president	John G. Speliopoulos
secretary	Gregory O. Theos
treasurer	George A. Telegas
council members	Augustine C. Chrysostom, Harry P. Demos, Andrew F. Lawandales, Frank H. Panegeris, Milton D. Stratos, Theodore A. Tsiropoulos, Nicholas J. Zervos

1960	
president	Paul J. Gelegotis
vice-president	Gregory O. Theos
secretary	Augustine C. Chrysostom
treasurer	George A. Telegas

council members	Angelo A. Anastopoulo, Arthur N. Corontzes, Arthur (Art) S. Homer, Frank H. Panegeris, Harry G. Speliopoulos Spell, Milton D. Stratos, Theodore A. Tsiropoulos

1961	
president	Milton D. Stratos
vice-president	Harry G. Speliopoulos Spell
secretary	Augustine C. Chrysostom
treasurer	Nicholas J. Theos
council members	George D. Bazakas, Kerry D. Gionis, Andrew F. Lawandales, Happy N. Lempesis, John C. Stamatiades, George A. Telegas, Gregory O. Theos

1962	
president	Gregory O. Theos
vice-president	Nicholas J. Theos
secretary	Kerry D. Gionis
treasurer	John C. Stamatiades
council members	George D. Bazakas, Peter Demos Jr., George C. Fassuliotis, Arthur (Art) S. Homer, Happy N. Lempesis, Constantine (Dino) J. Manos, George A. Telegas

1963	
president	Gregory O. Theos
vice-president	Arthur (Art) S. Homer
secretary	George C. Fassuliotis
treasurer	George S. Croffead
council members	George D. Bazakas, Andrew N. Christopoulo, Peter Demos Jr., Happy N. Lempesis, Andrew (Andy) L. Melissas, Emanuel S. Redman, Pete A. Yatrelis

1964	
president	Arthur (Art) S. Homer
vice-president	George C. Fassuliotis

secretary	William A. Larry
treasurer	Andrew (Andy) L. Melissas
council members	George D. Bazakas, Andrew N. Christopoulo, George S. Croffead, Harry G. Hitopoulos, Eleas F. Lawandales, Emanuel S. Redman, Pete A. Yatrelis

1965	
president	Andrew (Andy) L. Melissas
vice-president	George S. Croffead
secretary	George C. Fassuliotis
treasurer	Andrew N. Christopoulo
council members	George D. Bazakas, Harry G. Hitopoulos, Arthur (Art) S. Homer, William A. Larry, Eleas F. Lawandales, Andrew P. Leventis, Pete A. Yatrelis

1966	
president	Andrew (Andy) L. Melissas
vice-president	George S. Croffead
secretary	Harry G. Hitopoulos
treasurer	Andrew N. Christopoulo
council members	George D. Bazakas, James P. Demetre, Andrew P. Leventis, Emanuel G. Malanos, Constantine (Dino) J. Manos, John B. Marcus, Pete A. Yatrelis

1967	
president	George S. Croffead
vice-president	Harry G. Hitopoulos
secretary	James P. Demetre
treasurer	George D. Bazakas
(OK)	Andrew N. Christopoulo, treasurer, replaced by Socrates P. Creticos, Pat C. Gazes
(OKC)	Emanuel G. Malanos, Constantine (Dino) J. Manos, John B. Marcus, Andrew (Andy) L. Melissas, Pete A. Yatrelis

1968	
president	George S. Croffead
vice-president	Harry G. Hitopoulos

secretary	Constantine (Dino) J. Manos
treasurer	George D. Bazakas
council members	Socrates P. Creticos, Pat C. Gazes, Demetrios C. Liollio, John P. Manos, Andrew (Andy) L. Melissas, Stathy A. Tumboli, Pete A. Yatrelis

1969	
president	Harry G. Hitopoulos
vice-president	Constantine (Dino) J. Manos
secretary	John P. Manos
treasurer	Demetrios C. Liollio
council members	Socrates P. Creticos, George S. Croffead, John G. Gatgounis, Anthony N. Pappas, Angelo E. Stoucker, Stathy A. Tumboli, Nicholas J. Zervos

1970	
president	Constantine (Dino) J. Manos
vice-president	Anthony N. Pappas
secretary	Peter J. Zervos
treasurer	Angelo E. Stoucker
council members	George S. Croffead, John G. Gatgounis, John G. Kanellos, Demetrios C. Liollo, John J. Manos, John W. Perry replaced by John C. Chrysostom, John C. Chrysostom replaced by Athanas T. Tsiropoulos, Nicholas J. Zervos

1971	
president	Nicholas J. Zervos
vice-president	John J. Manos
secretary	Toula S. Latto
treasurer	Peter J. Zervos
council members	Spero N. Drake, Urania Tumboli Ferrara, John G. Kanellos, Demetrios C. Liollio, Constantine (Dino) J. Manos, Demetrious (Jimmy) N. Palassis, Athanas T. Tsiropoulos

1972	
president	Nicholas J. Zervos
vice-president	Theofanis (Ted) N. Gianaris
secretary	Toula S. Latto
treasurer	Theodore A. Tsiropoulos
council members	Elliott A. Constantine, Spero N. Drake, Urania Tumboli Ferrara replaced by Peter J. Zervos, John G. Gatgounis, George S. Niketas, Demetrious (Jimmy) N. Palassis, Nicholas J. Theos

1973	
president	John G. Gatgounis
vice-president	John B. Carroll
secretary	Elliott A. Contantine
treasurer	Theodore A. Tsiropoulos
council members	Eleas F. Lawandales replaced Nicholas J. Theos, Jerry M. Jackis replaced by Eleas F. Lawandales, Theofanis (Ted) N. Gianaris (vice-president) replaced by Constantine N. Palassis, Arthur (Art) S. Homer, Mike A. Magoulas, George J. Morris, George S. Niketas, Chris A. Zecopoulos (John B. Carroll elected vice-president)

1974	
president	Mike A. Magoulas
vice-president	Hugh W. Ford
secretary	Thomas G. Croffead
treasurer	John B. Carroll
council members	Arthur (Art) S. Homer replaced by George S. Croffead, Jerry M. Jackis replaced by Steve A. Palassis, William H. Koss replaced by James L. Strobel, George J. Morris, Constantine N. Palassis, Emanuel S. Redman, Chris A. Zecopoulos

1975	
president	George J. Morris
vice-president	Thomas G. Croffead

secretary	James L. Strobel
treasurer	Mike A. Magoulas
council members	John H. Chakides, George S. Croffead, Hugh W. Ford replaced by William H. Koss, Constantine N. Palassis, Steve A. Palassis, Emanuel S. Redman, Harry G. Speliopoulos Spell

1976	
president	George J. Morris
vice-president	Thomas G. Croffead
secretary	James L. Strobel
treasurer	Mike A. Magoulas
council members	Kyriakos S. Aslanidis, John H. Chakides, George S. Croffead, Arthur (Art) S. Homer, Steve A. Palassis, Toula A. Pappas, Harry G. Speliopoulos Spell

1977	
president	Thomas G. Croffead
vice-president	Arthur (Art) S. Homer
secretary	Toula A. Pappas
treasurer	Gregory O. Theos
council members	Kyriakos S. Aslanidis, Chris J. Kapetanakos, George J. Kefalos, Effie A. Latto, Steve A. Palassis, James L. Strobel replaced by Milton D. Stratos, Chris A. Zecopoulos

1978	
president	Harry G. Hitopoulos
vice-president	Chris A. Zecopoulos
secretary	Toula Pappas Magoulas
treasurer	Jerry P. Gazes
council members	Arthur (Art) S. Homer, Chris J. Kapetanakos, George J. Kefalos, William H. Koss, Effie A. Latto, Steve A. Palassis, Gregory O. Theos

1979	
president	Harry G. Hitopoulos

vice-president	Jerry P. Gazes
secretary	Toula Pappas Magoulas replaced by Happy N. Lempesis
treasurer	Theodore A. Tsiropoulos
council members	John B. Carroll, Elliott A. Constantine, George S. Croffead, Arthur (Art) S. Homer replaced by Isidore C. Christ, William H. Koss replaced by Kyriakos S. Aslanidis, George J. Morris, Steve A. Palassis replaced by James V. Springer

1980	
president	George J. Morris
vice-president	Jerry P. Gazes
secretary	Kyriakos S. Aslanidis
treasurer	Theodore A. Tsiropoulos
council members	John B. Carroll, Isidore C. Christ, Elliott A. Constantine, Costa P. DeLuca, George S. Croffead, Happy N. Lempesis, James V. Springer

1981	
president	George J. Morris
vice-president	Kyriakos S. Aslanidis replaced by Harry G. Hitopoulos
secretary	Costa P. DeLuca
treasurer	Jerry P. Gazes
council members	John H. Chakides, Isidore C. Christ, Elliott A. Constantine, James C. Gazes, Chris J. Kapetanakos, Happy N. Lempesis, James V. Springer

1982	
president	George J. Morris
vice-president	John H. Chakides
secretary	Chris J. Kapetanakos
treasurer	Anthony J. Tellis
council members	Ronald D. Butler, Isidore C. Christ, Elliott A. Constantine replaced by Chris M. Stefanou, James C. Gazes, Harry G. Hitopoulos replaced by Raymond C. Geiger, Happy N. Lempesis, James V. Springer

1983	
president	George J. Morris
vice-president	Raymond C. Geiger
secretary	Chris J. Kapetanakos
treasurer	Anthony J. Tellis
council members	Ronald D. Butler, Isidore C. Christ, James C. Gazes, Dennis A. Kambitsis, Happy N. Lempesis, James V. Springer, Chris M. Stefanou

1984	
president	George J. Morris
vice-president	John H. Chakides
secretary	Chris J. Kapetanakos
treasurer	Chris A. Zecopoulos
council members	Ron D. Butler, James C. Gazes, Raymond C. Geiger, Jimmie A. Gianoukos, Dennis A. Kambitsis, George E. Scordalakis, Chris M. Stefanou

1985	
president	Raymond C. Geiger
vice-president	John H. Chakides
secretary	Chris M. Stefanou
treasurer	Dennis A. Kambitsis
council members	Ron D. Butler, Isidore C. Christ, James C. Gazes, Jimmie A. Gianoukos, James P. Kordonis, George E. Scordalakis replaced by Harry G. Speliopoulos Spell, Chris A. Zecopoulos

1986	
president	Raymond C. Geiger
vice-president	Mike A. Magoulas
secretary	Chris M. Stefanou
treasurer	Dennis A. Kambitsis

council members	Ron D. Butler, James C. Gazes, Jimmie A. Gianoukos, James P. Kordonis, Harry G. Speliopoulos Spell replaced by William (Billy) P. Lempesis, James V. Springer filled vacancy May 15, 1986, Chris A. Zecopoulos replaced by Kyriakos S. Aslanidis

1987	
president	Raymond C. Geiger
vice-president	Mike A. Magoulas
secretary	Chris M. Stefanou
treasurer	Dennis A. Kambitsis
council members	Kyriakos S. Aslanidis, Ron D. Butler replaced by John Kontos, Jimmie A. Gianoukos, Larry T. Haley, James P. Kordonis, William (Billy) P. Lempesis, James V. Springer

1988	
president	Raymond C. Geiger
vice-president	George J. Morris
secretary	William (Billy) P. Lempesis
treasurer	Dennis A. Kambitsis
council members	Larry T. Haley, Chris J. Kapetanakos, John Kontos, James P. Kordonis, Thomas P. Meletis, James V. Springer, Chris M. Stefanou

1989	
president	George J. Morris
vice-president	Raymond C. Geiger
secretary	Dena J. Panos
treasurer	Dennis A. Kambitsis
council members	Chris J. Kapetanakos, John Kontos, William (Billy) P. Lempesis replaced by Happy N. Lempesis, Thomas P. Meletis, Chris M. Palles replaced by Mike A. Magoulas, Lucy Stupenos Spell, James V. Springer

1990	
president	George J. Morris
vice-president	Thomas P. Meletis
secretary	Dena J. Panos
treasurer	Dennis A. Kambitsis
council members	J. Michael J. Grayson, John Kontos, Thymie (Tim) Latto, Happy N. Lempesis, Mike A. Magoulas, Ross J. Moskos, Lucy Stupenos Spell

1991	
president	George J. Morris
vice-president	Raymond C. Geiger
secretary (acting)	J. Michael Grayson
council members	George N. Avgeropoulos, Spero J. Fokas, John Kontos, Thymie (Tim) S. Latto, Happy N. Lempesis, Thomas P. Meletis, Ross J. Moskos, Lucy Stupenos Spell

1992	
president	Thymie (Tim) S. Latto
vice-president	Lucy Stupenos Spell
secretary	Jay D. Rickman
treasurer	Victor K. Kliossis
council members	George N. Avgeropoulos, Spero J. Fokas, Raymond C. Geiger, Pano F. Kordonis, John J. Manos, Ross J. Moskos, George C. Zecopoulos

1993	
president	Thymie (Tim) S. Latto
vice-president	Pano F. Kordonis
secretary	Jay D. Rickman
treasurer	Victor K. Kliossis
council members	Demetrios G. Diasourakis, Mike A. Magoulos, John J. Manos, Ross J. Moskos, Demetrious (Jimmy) N. Palassis, Susan Zakis, George C. Zecopoulos replaced by George J. Morris

1994 (Sunday, March 13, 1994, a parish General Assembly votes to expand Parish Council from eleven members to fifteen)	
president	Hope Gazes Grayson
vice-president	Nicholas J. Clekis
secretary	Jimmie A. Gianoukos
treasurer	Victor K. Kliossis
assistant treasurer	Susan Zakis replaced by Ross J. Moskos
council members	John P. Alvanos, Paul J. Chrysostom, Peter Demos Jr., Demetrios G. Diasourakis, George C. Fassuliotis, Pano F. Kordonis replaced by Nicholas J. Theos, Mike A. Magoulas, George J. Morris, Demetrious (Jimmy) N. Palassis, Dianne Lempesis Rustin

1995	
president	George J. Morris
vice-president	Jimmie A.Gianoukos
secretary	Dianne Lempesis Rustin
treasurer	Kerry D. Gionis
council members	John P. Alvanos, Paul J. Chrysostom, Nicholas J. Clekis, Peter Demos Jr., Kiki Slemp Diasourakis, George C. Fassuliotis, Hope Gazes Grayson replaced by Thomas G. Croffead, Victor K. Kliossis, Thymie (Tim) S. Latto, Jay D. Rickman, Nicholas J. Theos

1996	
president	Peter Demos Jr.
vice-president	Jimmie A. Gianoukos
secretary	James Kalafatis
treasurer	Toula S. Latto
assistant treasurer	Kiki Slemp Diasourakis
council members	Brenda Kimball Alvanos, John P. Alvanos, Louis (Lou) Anderson, Kerry D. Gionis, Thymie (Tim) S. Latto, Jay D. Rickman, Dianne Lempesis Rustin, Nicholas J. Theos, Lena Kordonis Vozikis, Peter J. Zervos

1997	
president	Jimmie A. Gianoukos
vice-president	Peter Demos Jr.
secretary	James Kalafatis
treasurer	Toula S. Latto
assistant treasurer	Kiki Slemp Diasourakis
council members	Brenda Kimball Alvanos, John P. Alvanos, Louis (Lou) Anderson, Helen Koziares Fassuliotis, Kerry D. Gionis, Sam S. Howell, Mary Lee Demetre Lavelle, Dianne Lempesis Rustin, Nicholas J. Theos, Peter J. Zervos

1998	
president	Peter Demos Jr.
vice-president	Helen Koziares Fassuliotis
secretary	Dena J. Panos
treasurer	Charles G. Demetriades
assistant treasurer	Kiki Slemp Diasourakis
council members	Demetrios G. Diasourakis, Michael (Mike) J. Dupree, Kerry D. Gionis, Sam S. Howell, Mary Lee Demetre Lavelle, Basil W. Lefter, George J. Morris, Theodore L. Pappas, Nicholas J. Theos

1999	
president	Helen Koziares Fassuliotis
vice-president	Susan Zakis
secretary	Dena J. Panos
treasurer	Peter Demos Jr.
assistant treasurer	John G. Kanellos
council members	Sophia Lawandales Demos, Demetrios G. Diasourakis, Michael (Mike) J. Dupree, Mary Lee Demetre Lavelle, Basil W. Lefter, George J. Morris, George Pappas, Theodore L. Pappas, John Stoner, Nicholas J. Theos replaced by Chris C. Zecopoulos

2000	
president	Helen Koziares Fassuliotis

vice-president	Susan Zakis
secretary	Dena J. Panos
treasurer	Peter Demos Jr.
assistant treasurer	John G. Kanellos
council members	Robert R. Albanese, Sophia Lawandales Demos, Michael (Mike) J. Dupree, Thymie (Tim) S. Latto, Mary Lee Demetre Lavelle, George Pappas replaced by George J. Morris, Theodore L. Pappas, Harry G. Speliopoulos Spell, John Stoner, Chris C. Zecopoulos

2001	
president	Helen Koziares Fassuliotis
vice-president	Susan Zakis
recording secretary	Theodore L. Pappas
corresponding secretary	Thymie (Tim) S. Latto
treasurer	Dena J. Panos
assistant treasurer	John G. Kanellos
council members	Robert R. Albanese, John P. Alvanos, Peter Demos Jr., Sophia Lawandales Demos, Michael (Mike) J. Dupree, Mary Lee Demetre Lavelle, George J. Morris, Harry G. Speliopoulos Spell, Chris C. Zecopoulos

2002	
president	Helen Koziares Fassuliotis
vice-president	Susan Zakis
recording secretary	Theodore L. Pappas
corresponding secretary	Thymie (Tim) S. Latto
treasurer	Dena J. Panos
assistant treasurer	John G. Kanellos
council members	Robert R. Albanese, John P. Alvanos, Peter Demos Jr., Sophia Lawandales Demos, Connie Filippopoulou, Mary Lee Demetre Lavelle, George J. Morris, George Yankovich, Melva Zinaich

2003	
president	Helen Koziares Fassuliotis

vice-president	Mary Lee Demetre Lavelle
recording secretary	Theodore L. Pappas
corresponding secretary	Thymie (Tim) S. Latto
treasurer	Dena J. Panos
assistant treasurer	Melva Zinaich
council members	Robert R. Albanese, Peter Demos Jr., Sophia Lawandales Demos, Connie Filippopoulou, Kerry D. Gionis, George E. Malanos, George J. Morris, James Patenaude, George Yankovich

2004	
president	Mary Lee Demetre Lavelle
vice-president	Theodore L. Pappas
recording secretary	Hamilton (Hammie) Rodman Kanellos
corresponding secretary	George J. Morris
treasurer	Cynthia Cadell Alvanos
assistant treasurer	Sophia Lawandales Demos
council members	John P. Alvanos, Peter Demos Jr., Helen Koziares Fassuliotis, William W. Frehse Jr., Kerry D. Gionis, Demetre A. Homer, George E. Malanos, James Patenaude, Melva Zinaich

2005 (October 30, 2005, bylaws are approved by a parish General Assembly, which include a change in Parish Council members from fifteen back to the original eleven. This change is eased in over a two-year time frame)	
president	Mary Lee Demetre Lavelle
vice-president	Theodore L. Pappas
recording secretary	Hamilton (Hammie) Rodman Kanellos
corresponding secretary	George J. Morris
treasurer	Cynthia Cadell Alvanos
assistant treasurer	Sophia Lawandales Demos
council members	John P. Alvanos, Harriet Borom, Peter Demos Jr., Laurie Elliott Milligan, Helen Koziares Fassuliotis, William W. Frehse Jr., Demetre A. Homer, George E. Malanos, Melva Zinaich

2006	
president	Mary Lee Demetre Lavelle
vice-president	Harry G. Hitopoulos
recording secretary	Hamilton (Hammie) Rodman Kanellos
corresponding secretary	George J. Morris
treasurer	Cynthia Cadell Alvanos
assistant treasurer	Sophia Lawandales Demos
council members	Robert R. Albanese, Harriet Borom, Laurie Elliott Milligan, Helen Koziares Fassuliotis, William W. Freshe Jr., Joey L. Hammond, George E. Malanos

2007	
president	Mary Lee Demetre Lavelle
vice-president	Sam S. Howell
recording secretary	Hamilton (Hammie) Rodman Kanellos
treasurer	William W. Frehse Jr.
assistant treasurer	Sophia Lawandales Demos
council members	Robert R. Albanese, Cynthia Cadell Alvanos, Helen Koziares Fassuliotis filled vacancy due to death of vice-president Harry G. Hitopoulos, Joey L. Hammond, George E. Malanos, Jeff J. Ritchey replaced Cynthia Cadell Alvanos, Melva Zinaich

2008	
president	Mary Lee P. Demetre Lavelle
vice-president	Sam S. Howell
secretary	Jeff J. Ritchey
treasurer	Victor K. Kliossis
assistant treasurer	Sophia Lawandales Demos
council members	Helen Koziares Fassuliotis, William W. Freshe Jr., Joey L. Hammond, George E. Malanos, Effie Latto Meletis, Melva Zinaich

PARISH SECRETARIES

When the church was established in 1910, the secretary of the Parish Council took care of all matters pertaining to the parish and of the different committees up until 1946, when the parish hired John Chrysostom as the Greek School teacher and secretary. The official minutes of the Parish Council were written in the Greek language until the 1950s.

1946–1948	John C. Chrysostom
September 1948–December 31, 1953	Gus S. Ballis
January 1, 1954–October 3, 1993	Rosa P. Paulatos
January 1994–April 1995	Estacia Redman Thompson
April 1995–February 1996	Patrick J. Murphy
February 1996–January 21, 1997	Debbie Spitler
April 1997–June 20, 1997	Brenda Heldreth
June 24, 1997–June 19, 2002	Emily Lacey
June 24, 2002–August 14, 2002	Lindsey Laughlan
August 15, 2002–October 15, 2002	Jeannett Rourk
January 28, 2003–May 28, 2003	Elizabeth Morgan, Louise Gladden, assistant
May 19, 2003–November 11, 2003	Jane Dawson
October 27, 2003–present	Carol Jones Wenner

SUNDAY SCHOOL DIRECTORS AND ASSISTANTS

Eclecte A. Tsiropoulos, 1948–50 (assistant)
Lula Gigis, 1951–53
Melba N. Kaleondgis, 1953–54
Penelope Gianaris, 1954–56
Rosa P. Paulatos, 1956–78, 1987–93
Betty L. Lawandales, 1978–80, 1980–81 (assistant)
Helen (Nitsa) Siokos Demos, 1978–79 (assistant)
Hope Gazes Grayson, 1979–1980 (assistant), 1980–87
Cathy Gazes, 1981–87 (assistant)
Mia G. Stamatiades, 1987–89 (assistant)
Valerie Walker Papadopoulos, 1989–94 (assistant)
Brenda Kimball Alvanos, 1994–2006 (assistant)
Darice Chocas Norton, 2005–06 (assistant)
Phylis Gates, 2006–07 (assistant)
Sylvia P. Trapalis, 2006–09

Lay Assistant
Daniel Carabus, 2006–present, Youth and Young Adult Ministries

Chapter 4

CHURCH-AFFILIATED
ORGANIZATIONS

THE GREEK LADIES PHILOPTOCHOS SOCIETY

The Greek Orthodox Ladies Philoptochos Society, the official philanthropic organization of the Greek Orthodox Church in America, was established in November 1931 by the late Ecumenical Patriarch Athenagoras I, who was then serving as Archbishop of North and South America.

The national program benefits a number of organizations and causes, including St. Basil's Academy; Hellenic College/Holy Cross School of Theology; Archdiocesan Missions; St. Photios Shrine in St. Augustine, Florida; UNICEF; and an emergency fund for victims of natural disasters. Programs include committees on AIDS, aging, homelessness, child abuse prevention, drug and alcohol abuse and child pornography. Its social work services and programs assist persons of all ages throughout the Archdiocese with issues of health, mental health, government entitlements, etc.

There are an estimated five hundred Philoptochos chapters in the United States, with more than twenty-seven thousand members as of 2007. The structure of the Philoptochos includes the National Board, Diocesan Boards and Chapters in every parish of the Archdiocese.

The first attempt to organize this society in Charleston was in 1931 by the Reverend Paraskevas Papatheophrastou, but this was unsuccessful. Later, in November of 1947, the Very Reverend Modestos Stavrides succeeded and the Philoptochos has since taken a leading part in the activities of the Charleston community. The presidents of the society known as the St. Irene Philoptochos Ladies Society from 1947 through 2009 are as follows:

1947–49	Chrysanthe (Chrysa) Varras Manos	**1978–79**	Georgia Pappas Croffead
1949–51	Fran Billias Lempesis	**1979–80**	Angie Demos Zervos
1951–53	Angeliki Athan Gianaris	**1980–81**	Alice Lambros Vagenas
1953–55	Helen Kaperonis Leventis	**1981–82**	Patricia Crosby Croffead
1955–57	Aphrodite Stevens Pappas	**1982–83**	Sophia Lawandales Demos
1957–59	Mary Poulos Pavlis	**1983–85**	Christine Savvas Homer
1959–61	Athena Critikos Gazes	**1985–87**	Sandra Croffead Veronee
1961–63	Effie Aliprantis Latto	**1987–88**	Anna Zangaris Corontzes
1963–65	Kathryn (Kay) Manos Leventis	**1988–90**	Helen Koziares Fassuliotis
1965–67	Katherine Gigis Theos	**1990–93**	Diane Stamas Mashead
1967–68	Katina Corontzes Manos	**1993–95**	Alexis Homer Glover
1968–69	Sophia Lawandales Demos	**1995–97**	Georgia Homer Darby
1969–71	Mary Gatgounis Larry	**1997–99**	Maria Corontzes Alfieris
1971–72	Mary Gigis Moskos	**1999–2001**	Georgette Karp Palassis
1972–73	Simone Kaleondgis Alvanos	**2001–03**	Deborah Demos Jonas
1973–75	Urania Tumboli Ferrara	**2003–05**	Gina Puelo Pappas
1975–76	Helen Kapsimalis Theos	**2005–07**	Erica Rouvalis
1976–77	Helen (Nitsa) Siokos Demos	**2007–09**	Renie A. Forsberg
1977–78	Patricia Crosby Croffead		

Chrysanthe (Chrysa) Varras Manos, first president of the Philoptochos Society, 1947–49.

Ladies' Auxiliary Council photo taken in the 1930s. Maria Chrisanthis Gianaris, Mnosto Rosopoulos Stamatiades, Fotine Armeo Panegeris, Demetra Gialetes Gonos, Viola Sterlakos Larry.

Philoptochos Society, 1951. *Front row*: Mrs. Georgia Banis Palassis, secretary; Mrs. Harritomeni Lambrianou Gigis, vice-president; Mrs. Fran Billias Lempesis, president; Mrs. Constance (Connie) Alexopoulos Misoyianis, treasurer. *Back row*: Mrs. Ismene Papadopoulos Gongos; Mrs. Antonia Palassis Magoulas; Mrs. Helen Gianatos Georgeo; and Mrs. Nina Delaporta Tumboli, all members of the Board of Directors.

The philanthropic goal of the society is expressed as follows: "To help the poor, the destitute, the hungry, the aged, the sick, the unemployed, the orphaned, the imprisoned, the widowed, the handicapped, the victims of natural disasters and to offer assistance to anyone who may need the help of the church."

The Charleston Chapter supports such charities as the Lowcountry Children's Center, Lowcountry Crisis Ministry, Hospice, Paracletis Greek Orthodox Monastery, Coastal Crisis Chaplaincy, VA Ministry, Ronald McDonald House, My Sister's House, Winwood Farm for Boys and UNICEF among other philanthropic needs.

THE COOKBOOK: *POPULAR GREEK RECIPES*

As the young wife of Father Nicholas C. Trivelas in 1950, Presvytera Despina Ross Trivelas presented an idea to the Philoptochos Society that the ladies compile a Greek-American cookbook. At that time, no one could imagine what a resounding success the cookbook would achieve.

In early 1950, during the Philoptochos presidency of Fran Billias Lempesis, a committee was organized to compile a Greek recipe book. Members were Helen Kasimatis Palassis, Nina Delaporta Tumboli, Constance (Connie) Alexopoulos Misoyianis, Voula Soufas Moskos and Presvytera Despina Ross Trivelas, who met weekly to consider recipes, make proper selections and test kitchen recipes.

In 1957, under the presidency of Aphrodite Stevens Pappas, the original cookbook committee was reestablished with new members, namely Fran Billias Lempesis, Joanna (Anna) Demos Latto and Katherine Carabatsos Gianoukos, to prepare a book for a printer. Prologues for each chapter were written by Eva A. Tsiropoulos and Presvytera Despina Ross Trivelas, drawings were made by Sophia P. Paulatos and Costan D. Pappas. Typing of the original cookbook and for the second printing was done by Rosa P. Paulatos. The printing on the cover of the cookbook, as well as the headings of each chapter page, were originated and hand printed by Father Nicholas C. Trivelas to resemble the Grecian style.

The first printing, for five hundred books, was published in 1957. At that time there were perhaps only three Greek-American cookbooks, produced by communities in Tarpon Springs, Florida; Manchester, New Hampshire; and Detroit, Michigan. For promotion, the society mailed circulars to every Greek community in the country and ads were periodically placed in the *Orthodox Observer*, the newspaper for the Greek Orthodox Church in America.

By 1965, the cookbook was enjoying tremendous success, with orders coming in from all over the country. An additional one hundred recipes were added, with Presvytera Despina Ross Trivelas writing menus for fasting, Helen Malis Theos preparing the new improved index and Mary Gigis Moskos retyping the cookbook with all the new additions. Dr. John J. Manos was consulted to validate the nutritional value of the menus for fasting. The cookbook is a showcase of Greek-American cuisine, with many recipes cooked in olive oil, meat and fish with lemon and olive oil, salads with feta cheese and

Presvytera Despina Ross Trivelas, originator of the cookbook.

seasonings such as parsley, dill and oregano. This Mediterranean cuisine has grown ever more popular through the years in America.

In 1976, the cookbook was again revised by Helen (Nitsa) Siokos Demos, Angie Demos Zervos, Helen Malis Theos, Mary Gigis Moskos, Presvytera Despina Ross Trivelas and Katina Corontzes Manos, with many new recipes included. Antonia (Toni) Manos added sketches to the pages.

In February 1977, President Helen (Nitsa) Siokos Demos wrote the *Ladies' Home Journal* and sent them a copy of the book. The magazine choose this book for its community cookbook series, and representatives of *Ladies' Home Journal* arrived in Charleston to interview the ladies for a feature in their magazine, which was published in the February 1978 issue. From this national exposure, the Philoptochos received thousands of orders for quite a long time. From humble beginnings, the cookbook project matured into a viable business, with books sent all over the world including France, other parts of Europe, South Africa, South America, Canada and the Bahamas.

Sophia Lawandales Demos has acted as cookbook treasurer and Mary Gatgounis Larry has acted as distribution chairman, writing letters to large department stores, television editors, churches and newly opened stores.

In January 2003, a new chapter, "Popular Greek Recipes," was added, with sixty new recipes and mealtime prayers. This new section includes many traditional recipes with familiar procedures and others with new adaptations.

Commemorating the fiftieth anniversary of the cookbook (1957–2007), an anniversary edition has been published in hardback as a result of the dedication and resourcefulness of the cookbook committee. In 2007, the cookbook was also awarded the Tabasco

Community Cookbook Award as the Walter S. McIlhenny Hall of Fame Winner, which honors books considered classic in their field. The award is given to recognize uniquely American books published for fundraising purposes by nonprofit organizations and honors the efforts of volunteers who use it effectively to benefit charitable endeavors. Only cookbooks that have sold more than 100,000 copies are eligible for this honor. As of 2007, only sixty-two books had been awarded this distinction. The honorees receive award stickers to be placed on the book. The cookbook is one of the most popular Greek cookbooks in the marketplace.

Over 110,000 cookbooks have been printed. The Philoptochos Society has used these profits not only for the benefit of the local Greek community, but has also provided substantial funds for various charitable organizations such as Horizon House for delinquent children and the Medical University Children's Hospital.[27]

GREEK ORTHODOX YOUTH OF AMERICA (GOYA)

The Greek Orthodox Youth of America is a federated organization of the Greek Orthodox Archdiocese of America, with youth organizations in each parish in the United States. In Charleston, this effort was undertaken in 1951 by J. Louis Lempesis, who was designated to attend a meeting in Charlotte, North Carolina, for this purpose. Thereafter, with the concurrence of the Parish Council and under the direction of Father Nicholas C. Trivelas, Georgia P. Leventis, Margaret N. Klonaris, Dia G. Misoyianis, Stella J. Moskos, Elias S. Latto, Constan J. Moskos, Ernest A. Babanats, George P. Saclarides and Costan A. Magoulas met to study the possibility of organizing the GOYA in Charleston.

An organizational meeting was held October 13, 1953, at the Hellenic Community Center. The Charleston GOYA Chapter was officially and formally organized October 27, 1953, with Peter W. Lempesis as president, Constan (Connie) J. Moskos as vice-president, Joan A. Carabatsos as secretary and Andrew F. Lawandales as treasurer.[28]

In November 1959, the Parish Council granted permission to Father Nicholas C. Trivelas to organize a Junior Greek Orthodox Youth of America for boys and girls ages twelve through seventeen. The first youth director was Chrysanthe Varras Manos. The program for the Junior GOYA was the same as the senior organization, which included religious, educational, athletic and social activities. The first board had John W. Anagnos as its president, Nena C. Horton as secretary and Theodore J. Manos as treasurer. The Junior GOYA is now known as the GOYA, and in 1965 the senior group changed the name to St. Luke's Fellowship, which is no longer in existence.

The GOYANS have supported the church, its festivals and other endeavors, and some youth have dressed in traditional Greek costumes to demonstrate the Greek folk dances to the Charleston community. More recently, youth calling themselves Hellas Dancers are under the direction of Eleni Apostolakis Hopes. Eleni is originally from Chicago, Illinois, where she attended Roosevelt University Chicago Musical College and studied classical ballet and Spanish dance and is considered a dance master. She has traveled throughout Greece studying and collecting information to share and teach the Greek Americans

Representative GOYANS, 1962. *Back row*: Arthur (Art) S. Homer, Kerry D. Gionis, Father Nicholas C. Trivelas. *Middle row*: Kathryn (Kay) Manos Leventis, Cleo G. Kanellos. *Front row*: Alexandra P. Demos, Rosa P. Paulatos, Sophia P. Paulatos, Katina W. Lempesis.

about their Greek heritage through music and dance. She teaches Holy Trinity's youth, ages five and up, with the GOYANS participating in the annual dance competition with youth from other parishes in the Diocese. The participants wear authentic Greek costumes all sewn by Eleni. She was awarded three gold medals from the Diocese for her costumes and the dancers won a silver medal during the 2005 competition and another silver medal during the 2008 dance competition from the Diocese.

Chapter 5

GREEK AMERICAN ORGANIZATIONS

AMERICAN HELLENIC EDUCATIONAL PROGRESSIVE ASSOCIATION (AHEPA)

The Order of AHEPA (American Hellenic Educational Progressive Association) was founded in Atlanta, Georgia, on July 26, 1922, to promote good citizenship and worthy civic endeavors. The eight founders conceived the idea of the establishment of an organization mainly of citizens of Greek descent, although not limited only to such members. During the organization's first year, from July 26, 1922, through October 15, 1923, thirty-two subordinate lodges were established and thirteen hundred members were initiated. These subordinate lodges were as follows:

1. Atlanta, GA
2. Charlotte, NC
3. Birmingham, AL
4. Charleston, SC
5. Savannah, GA
6. Jacksonville, FL
7. Memphis, TN
8. Shreveport, LA
9. Fayetteville, NC
10. Raleigh, NC
11. Wilson, NC
12. Tampa, FL
13. Tulsa, OK
14. Miami, FL
15. St. Petersburg, FL
16. Tarpon Springs, FL
17. St. Augustine, FL
18. West Palm Beach, FL
19. Fort Worth, TX
20. Dallas, TX
21. Fort Smith, AR
22. El Dorado, AR
23. Montgomery, AL
24. Boston, MA
25. New York City, NY
26. Philadelphia, PA
27. Muskogee, OK
28. Asheville, NC
29. Houston, TX
30. Baltimore, MD
31. Washington, D.C.
32. Winston-Salem, NC

First Annual Convention of the Fourteenth District Order of AHEPA, July 10–12, 1932, under auspices of Plato Chapter No. 4, Charleston, South Carolina. This picture was taken in front of the original Greek Orthodox church.

The AHEPA, with its programs of Americanism, the use of the English language and its assertion of being nonpolitical and nonsectarian, struck many Greek Americans as being heretical and it was bitterly criticized in many quarters, including the Greek newspapers in America. This criticism may be understandable because most Greek immigrants did not leave Greece because of political oppression or because of dissatisfaction with their government. They were patriotic citizens of that country, but they left for economic reasons and for work so that they could send money back to their families and relatives in the villages and return one day with funds to make better lives in Greece. Although probably most Greek immigrants had, by the year 1922, decided that America was now their homeland and here they would stay, there were many who still fondly dreamed of returning to Greece. Consequently, the principles of AHEPA rankled and seemed revolutionary to some, and they felt resentment for an association that was trying to "Americanize the Greek."[29]

The first meeting of the Charleston Chapter of AHEPA was held in the Chamber of Commerce Building on Broad Street on January 28, 1923, when the late Eleftherios Venizelos, a prominent Greek political leader who was present at that meeting, offered to the Plato Chapter the Greek flag as a symbol of the friendliness between the two nations. The flag later was presented by the Chapter to the State of South Carolina.

Above: Banquet of Plato Chapter No. 4, Order of AHEPA, Charleston, South Carolina, May 13, 1923, held at the Crystal Restaurant located near the corner of Meeting and Society Streets. George John Speliopoulos and Pindaros (Pete) Chrisanthis, proprietors.

Below: Early photograph of AHEPA members in their full regalia.

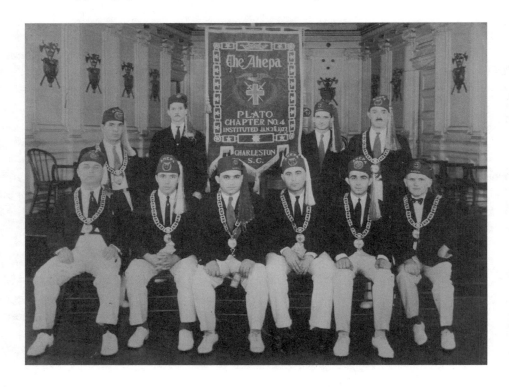

Greek classics donated by AHEPA to The Citadel. *Left to right*: Arthur N. Corontzes, The Citadel librarian; John C. Stamatiades; General Mark W. Clark; Andrew P. Leventis; Gregory O. Theos.

AHEPA Membership Awards. Harry G. Speliopoulos Spell, president (1971). *First row*: John P. Liatos, Nicholas H. Gianaris, Peter D. Demetre, Athanas T. Tsiropoulos, William Logothetis. *Second row*: Harry P. Demos, Andrew A. Trapalis, Alex G. Tumboli, George A. Telegas, George M. Billias. *Third row*: Nick A. Tsiropoulos, George D. Bazakas, Pete N. (Papaphilippou) Philipps, George C. Kanellos, Theodore A. Tsiropoulos.

Picture of members of AHEPA taken in 1961 in front of AHEPA house. *First row*: Harry G. Speliopoulos Spell, Arthur (Art) S. Homer, John G. Speliopoulos. *Second row*: Emanuel S. Redman, Peter W. Lempesis, George P. Stamatiades, Anthony (Tony) D. Gianoukos, John G. Misoyianis. *Also pictured*: Angelo A. Anastopoulo, Marion A. Latto, Nicholas A. Pappas, Dr. George S. Croffead, Anthony (Tony) J. Tellis, George N. Gianaris, Harry N. Gianaris, James P. Demetre, Peter D. Demetre, George Bouzos, Harry P. Demos, George D. Bazakas, George A. Telegas, Pete N. (Papaphilippou) Philipps, Andrew A. Trapalis, Athanas T. Tsiropoulos, George Manos, John B. Marcus, Alex G. Tumboli, Tom S. Haley.

Periclean Award given to Governor James B. Edwards by AHEPA. *Left to right*: Steve G. Moskos, Alex G. Tumboli, Governor Edwards, Peter D. DeLuca and John G. Speliopoulos.

The Charleston Chapter, known as Plato Chapter No. 4, had the following charter members, as their names appear on the charter issued September 17, 1923:

C.M. Cockinos	G. Kiritais	G. Gounos
F.M. Cockinos	N. Kaliondgis	P. Demos
G. Panouchopoulos	C. Valianatos	W.F. Gholson
N. Gianaris	A. Trapalis	N. Lempessis
T. Gianaris	F. Panigiris	S. Kokinnos
H. Demos	G. Mozakis	D. Gionis
T. Hadgi	G. Terlengas	P. Yangopoulos
P. Chrisanthou	P. Manos	T.P. Stoney
G. Morakis	W. Lempessis	T. Efstathiou
A. Tsiropoulos	C. Trapalis	J. Rousso
N. Tumboli	N. Varinos	N. Nickiforakis
G. Christopoulos	J. Liatos	T. Lambrakis
J. Gianaris	T. Carousos	T. Contozoglou
P. Pipergone	G. Savopoulos	J.E. Carris
S. Savopoulos	P. Christanthis	J. Larry
N. Panachopoulos	A. Tumboli	W.T. Davis
Kalanthas	G. Phillips	

The first president of the Chapter was Costas Cockinos. Past presidents of the Chapter and their dates of service are as follows:

C.M. Cockinos	1923–24	2 terms
Athanas T. Tsiropoulos	1925–26	2 terms
Nick H. Gianaris	1927	1 term
Harry P. Demos	1928	1 term
John P. Liatos	1929–30	2 terms
William J. Logothetis	1931–32	2 terms
John T. Chakeris	1933	1 term
Peter P. Demos	1934	1 term
Angelo J. Castanes	1935	1 term
Theodore Gianaris	1936	1 term
Diasouris D. Diasourakis	1937	1 term
James H. Gianaris	1938–39	2 terms
Vasilios T. Voutsas	1940–41	2 terms
Angelo G. Drakos	1942–43	2 terms
Fred Chacharonis	1944–46	3 terms
John Valassakis	1947	1 term

Thomas G. Pappas	1948	1 term
James P. Leventis	1949	1 term
Theodore A. Tsiropoulos	1950	1 term
Charles P. Trapalis	1951–52	2 terms
William J. Logothetis	1953–55	3 terms
Angelo A. Anastopoulo	1956–58	3 terms
Nick A. Tsiropoulos	1959–60	2 terms
Steve G. Moskos	1961 (Jan–June)	
Anthony (Tony) J. Tellis	1961 (July–Dec.)	
Andrew P. Leventis	1962	1 term
John G. Speliopoulos	1963	1 term
Stanley E. Georgeo	1964–65	2 terms
John G. Misoyianis	1966	1 term
Arthur (Art) S. Homer	1967	1 term
Emanuel S. Redman	1968–69	2 terms
Steve G. Moskos	1970	1 term
Harry G. Speliopoulos Spell	1971	1 term
John B. Carroll	1972	1 term
George J. Morris	1973–74	2 terms
Peter D. DeLuca	1975–76	2 terms
Mike A. Magoulas	1977–78	2 terms
Chris J. Kapetanakos	1979	1 term
John G. Speliopoulos	1980–81	2 terms
William H. Koss	1982–83	2 terms
Ted N. Gianaris	1984–85	2 terms
Jimmie A. Gianoukos	1986–87	2 terms
Leon A. Melissas	1988–89	2 terms
Telis C. Zecopoulos	1990–92	2 terms
Johnny C. Zecopoulos	1993–94	2 terms
Harry G. Speliopoulos Spell	1995	1 term
George J. Morris	1996	1 term
Steve G. Moskos	1997–2001	5 terms
Telis C. Zecopoulos	2002–07	5 terms

District Governors from Charleston were:

William J. Logothetis	1937–38
Angelo A. Anastopoulo	1961–62
Steve G. Moskos	1963–64
John Stamatiades	1965–66
John G. Speliopoulos	1966–67
Chris J. Kapetanakos	2004–05

In 1965, the AHEPA purchased a home at 11 Race Street that was dedicated during the presidency of John Misoyianis. Meetings and social events were held at the home until 2005, when the Chapter sold the property to the Greek Orthodox Church of the Holy Trinity in Charleston for a sum substantially below its market value. These funds were set aside to be used for low-income senior citizens' housing to be erected in Charleston County, in keeping with the AHEPA's civic and charitable endeavors.

Additionally, through the auspices of Plato Chapter No. 4, a scholarship program known as the John G. Speliopoulos Memorial Scholarship was established, with the first scholarship being awarded in 1990. John Speliopoulos was a member of AHEPA for many years. He served as Chapter secretary, vice-president and president, as well as chairman of the Board of Governors. He held the position of executive secretary of Plato Chapter No. 4 for twenty-five years. He was elected to district office in 1964 and served as District Governor in 1996–97. He was elected to the Supreme Lodge as Supreme Governor in 1971, becoming the first South Carolinian to serve on the Supreme Lodge.

Additionally, scholarships are awarded in memory of Anthony and Effie Maistrellis, who migrated to America from Asia Minor and who endowed these scholarships in gratitude to America for the opportunities it had given them. Furthermore, other scholarships have been awarded, one in memory of Milton D. Stratos, a successful businessman and prior president of the Parish Council of the Charleston Greek Orthodox Church. Another is awarded by Dr. Peter and Athena C. Gazes. Dr. Peter C. Gazes is a renowned cardiologist and distinguished professor of cardiology at the Medical University of South Carolina.[30] His wife, Athena, established the Reverend Nicholas C. Trivelas Library and Bookstore located at the Hellenic Community Center in Charleston in December 1992. An additional scholarship is awarded in memory of Margaret Gazes Morris, who was the first church organist for Holy Trinity Greek Orthodox Church in Charleston and the first woman of Greek descent to teach in the Charleston County public schools. A scholarship is awarded in the joint memory of Milton D. Stratos and Anna P. Stratos. This fund was established upon the passing of Anna, Milton's devoted wife. In 2006, a scholarship was established in memory of Angelo A. Anastopoulo by his son, Akim A. Anastopoulo. Angelo was a dedicated AHEPAN, having served as District Governor and, on the local level, as president of Plato Chapter No. 4, as well as in other capacities. Angelo was interested in political affairs and avidly supported democratic ideals. Over $100,000 in scholarships have been awarded as of 2007.

DAUGHTERS OF PENELOPE

The Daughters of Penelope is a women's auxiliary of the Order of AHEPA. The Daughters was founded on November 16, 1929, as an international educational and philanthropic organization. The Briseis Chapter Number 232 in Charleston was founded November 21, 1950. Mrs. Katherine Carabatsos Gianoukos was elected the first president of the Chapter. The aim of the Charleston Chapter is to promote social, ethical and intellectual interests of its members, to cultivate good citizenship and loyalty to America and to disseminate American-Hellenic culture. The other original officers included Kathryn (Kay) Manos Leventis, vice-president; Anna Manos Liatos, treasurer; and Katina N. Corontzes, secretary. Charter members were Joanna (Anna) Demos Latto, Antonia Christopoulou, Anna Christopher Gionis, Nina Delaporta Tumboli, Mary Moskos Mitchell, Voula Soufas Moskos, Helen W. Lefter, Helen Kasimatis Palassis, Olga Milonadakis Kanellos, Litsa Gregorakis Tumboli, Helen Canaris Moskos, Helen Papaharalambou Demos, Panagiota Alexopoulou Demos, Dia G. Misoyianis, Rosie P. Leventis and Lucille N. Christopoulou. The Daughters of Penelope donated the stained-glass window in the Narthex of the Holy Trinity Greek Orthodox Church in Charleston,

Daughters of Penelope, 1961. *Seated, front row*: Fran Billias Lempesis, Board of Governors; Anna Manos Liatos, treasurer; Simone Kaleondgis Alvanos, vice-president; Rosie Athens Anastopoulo, president; Vera J. Tellis, secretary; Katherine Kaldanis Drakos, Board of Governors. *Back row*: Georgia Pappas Croffead; Helen W. Lefter; Lythea Chakeris Gatgounis; Kathryn (Kay) Manos Leventis, Board of Governors, chairman; Christine Savvas Homer; Dia G. Misoyianis; Alexandra P. Demos; Anna Papageorge Stamatiades; Anna Christopher Gionis; Katina W. Lempesis. *Absent from picture*: Voula Soufas Moskos; Joanna (Anna) D. Latto; Helen Kapsimalis Theos; Athena Critikos Gazes; Lena Fletcher Moskos.

Daughters of Penelope, 1951. *Left to right*: Katina N. Corontzes, secretary; Mrs. Andrew (Kay) Leventis, vice-president; Katherine Carabatsos Gianoukos, president; Mrs. John P. Liatos, treasurer.

entitled Holy Trinity "Symbol 2." Otherwise, the Daughters have been very active in supporting the church and other philanthropic causes, including Penelope House, which is a shelter for battered women in Mobile, Alabama; My Sister's House, a shelter for battered women in Charleston; the University of Miami Comprehensive Cancer Center; AHEPA Bone Marrow Registry; and the fight against Cooley's anemia.

MAIDS OF ATHENS

The local Chapter of the Maids of Athens (Panathenians, Chapter Number 68) was organized in 1940, mainly through the efforts of Nicky Gazes. She attended a social affair in Memphis, Tennessee, in 1940, and was impressed with the Memphis Chapter of the Maids of Athens. On returning to Charleston, she contacted the then–District Governor of the Sons of Pericles, Stanley E. Georgeo, and the two of them proceeded to organize a Charleston Chapter. The Charleston Chapter, which is an auxiliary of the Order of AHEPA with young women as members, was active in civic as well as church

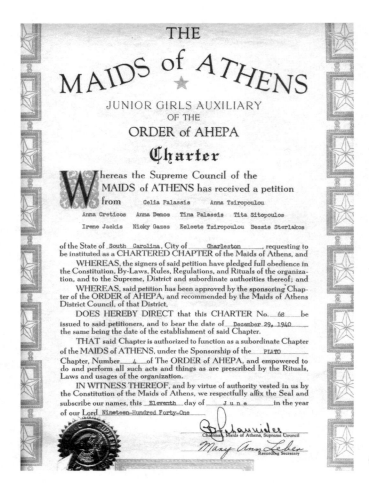

THE

MAIDS of ATHENS

JUNIOR GIRLS AUXILIARY
OF THE
ORDER of AHEPA

Charter

Whereas the Supreme Council of the MAIDS of ATHENS has received a petition from   Celia Palassis   Anna Tsiropoulou

Anna Creticos   Anna Demos   Tina Palassis   Tita Sitopoulos

Irene Jackis   Nicky Gazes   Eclecte Tsiropoulou   Bessie Sterlakos

of the State of __South Carolina__, City of _____Charleston_____, requesting to be instituted as a CHARTERED CHAPTER of the Maids of Athens, and

WHEREAS, the signers of said petition have pledged full obedience in the Constitution, By-Laws, Rules, Regulations, and Rituals of the organization, and to the Supreme, District and subordinate authorities thereof; and

WHEREAS, said petition has been approved by the sponsoring Chapter of the ORDER of AHEPA, and recommended by the Maids of Athens District Council, of that District,

DOES HEREBY DIRECT that this CHARTER No.__68__ be issued to said petitioners, and to bear the date of __December 29, 1940__ the same being the date of the establishment of said Chapter.

THAT said Chapter is authorized to function as a subordinate Chapter of the MAIDS of ATHENS, under the Sponsorship of the __PIATO__ Chapter, Number__4__of The ORDER of AHEPA, and empowered to do and perform all such acts and things as are prescribed by the Rituals, Laws and usages of the organization.

IN WITNESS THEREOF, and by virtue of authority vested in us by the Constitution of the Maids of Athens, we respectfully affix the Seal and subscribe our names, this __Eleventh__ day of ____June____ in the year of our Lord __Nineteen-Hundred Forty-One__

Chairman, Maids of Athens, Supreme Council

Mary Ann Leber
Recording Secretary

Charter of the Maids of Athens.

affairs. The group donated two beautiful stained-glass windows to the church, namely *Christ in Gethesemane* and *The Betrayal*, located in the upper dome level.

The first president of the Chapter was Eclecte A. Tsiropoulos. Nicky Gazes served as secretary and Tina R. Palassis served as treasurer. The founding members were Eclecte A. Tsiropoulos, Anna P. Creticos, Nicky Gazes, Irene M. Jackis, Tina R. Palassis, Celia A. Palassis, Bessie T. Sterlakos, Anna A. Tsiropoulos, Tico G. Hitopoulos and Joanna (Anna) J. Demos.

The Chapter participated in civic endeavors and also sponsored two Greek-language operettas, one in 1944 and one in 1946.

The Chapter president in 1953 was Ms. Katherine P. Gigis. The Chapter at that time had thirty-five members. Thereafter, the Chapter ceased to exist but was reorganized in 2006 and is now in existence. Although chartered as the Maids of Athens, it is now known as the Maids of Athena.

Maids of Athens, 1944. *Left to right*: Helen C. Davoulas, treasurer; Katherine A. Carabatsos, secretary; Nicky Gazes, vice-president; (standing) Irene M. Jackis, president.

Maids of Athens, 1951. *Seated*: Joan A. Carabatsos, executive secretary; Anna P. Chrisanthis, recording secretary. *Standing*: Katherine P. Gigis, vice-president; Mary T. Pappas, president; Alice J. Tellis, treasurer.

SONS OF PERICLES

The Sons of Pericles is a youth group and is an auxiliary of the Order of AHEPA. The Calhoun Chapter Number 74 was organized in 1932 by a group of ambitious boys of Greek descent. The installation of officers and the initiation of the original members was performed by the Savannah Chapter of the Sons of Pericles.

The first president of the Chapter was Elliott P. Botzis (1932), who later graduated from The Citadel and thereafter from the pharmacy school at the Medical University of South Carolina. He owned and operated Hampton Pharmacy on the corner of Rutledge Avenue and Cleveland Street for many years.[31]

Costa J. Rousso was president in 1933, Peter W. Lempesis in 1934, Marko J. Moskos in 1935 and George W. Lempesis in 1936.[32]

In 1936, the Chapter was dissolved. In 1942, it was again dissolved due to the draft, which had depleted its ranks. In 1948, through the efforts of James P. Leventis and Nick A. Tsiropoulos, the Chapter was reorganized with ten active members.

Early picture of the Sons of Pericles in the 1930s. *Left to right*: Costa J. Rousso, William (Bill) Campbell, Elliott P. Botzis, Peter W. Lempesis, George W. Lempesis, Thade Botzis, John Lempesis, Lonie Giatrakus, Peter Botzis, George N. Lempesis, George Theafratus, John P. Botzis.

Sons of Pericles, 1941. *First row*: Stanley E. Georgeo, John G. Misoyianis, Nick A. Tsiropoulos, Constan R. Palassis, Ernest Watkins, Jimmy D. Diasourakis. *Second row*: Pat C. Gazes, (in military uniform), Angelo P. Creticos, Socrates P. Creticos, John Marianos, Jerry G. Karapiparis (in military uniform), Ernest (Taso) G. Misoyianis. *Absent*: Demetrios (Jimmy) D. Diasourakis, Constan D. Diasourakis, George J. Moskos.

Sons of Pericles, 1944–45. *First row*: John G. Speliopoulos, Tommy G. Karapiparis. *Second row*: Jerry N. Drake, Gregg G. Hitopoulos, Nick C. Stamatiades, Themos C. Christ, William P. Chrisanthis.

Sons of Pericles, 1951. *Left to right*: Pano P. Lamis Jr., secretary; Panos J. Liatos, president; Nick J. Theos, vice-president; John W. Perry, treasurer.

One of the most outstanding members of the Chapter was Stanley E. Georgeo, who held the office of president for three consecutive years (1937–39). Ernest (Taso) G. Misoyianis was president in 1940–41, followed by Harry G. Speliopoulos Spell (1948), George P. Stamatiades (1949), Ross A. Magoulas (1950) and Panos J. Liatos (1951).

Stanley E. Georgeo was elected District Governor in 1940 and National Supreme Governor in 1941. Other persons who served as district officers were Andrew P. Leventis, governor (1942); George P. Stamatiades, secretary (1950); and Harry G. Speliopoulos Spell, treasurer (1951). Also on a national level, Edward J. Kiehling of Charleston served as a Supreme President in 1966. Nick Theodore of Greenville, who had an active association with the Charleston community and later served as lieutenant governor of South Carolina, was Supreme President in 1953–54.

One of the stained-glass windows of the Holy Trinity Church, *The Epiphany*, located in the upper dome windows, was donated by the Charleston Chapter.

In 1953, Stathy A. Tumboli was president with twenty-five active members. The Chapter is no longer active.

GREEK AMERICAN PROGRESSIVE ASSOCIATION (GAPA) AND OTHER ORGANIZATIONS

The Greek American Progressive Association (GAPA), in contradistinction to the AHEPA, placed its emphasis on being Greek as opposed to American, as the name reflects. Sparta Lodge Number 78 was the men's organization founded in Charleston February 2, 1929, and was part of the national GAPA organization that was formed

GAPA Sparta Lodge No. 78. *Left to right*: William J. Anagnos, secretary; Theodore C. Varras, president; Nick J. Drake, vice-president; James C. Manos, treasurer.

December 17, 1923. The founding officers were Theodore C. Varras, president; Nicholas J. Drake, vice-president; William J. Anagnos, secretary; and James C. Manos, treasurer. The board members were Efthimios D. Stamatelatos, Christ Pappas, Bob Thomas, Frank E. Lawandales and George C. Gonos. In 1934, the officers of the GAPA were D. Stephanatos, president; George G. Manos, vice-president; Theodore C. Varras, secretary; and Frank E. Lawandales, treasurer.

The ladies' auxiliary of GAPA was the oldest ladies' organization in the Greek community, having been organized in March 1933 with twenty charter members. It was formed due to the efforts of D. Stephanatos, Efthimios D. Stamatelatos and E. Chronis. The ladies' auxiliary, known as Anthousa Lodge Number 65, had as its first president Mrs. Effie Aliprantis Latto. The lodge was one of the most active in the nation and made many noteworthy financial contributions to the church, including the donation of one of the church Sanctuary stained-glass windows, entitled *Christ Blessing*. The ladies' auxiliary also undertook many philanthropic endeavors, such as assisting the American Red Cross. In 1934, the officers of the local GAPA Chapter were Mrs. Marista Zira Varvalides (Varras), president; Mrs. Demetra (Mitsa) Mavrantzakis Lawandales, vice-president; Mrs. Effie Alprantis Latto, secretary; and Mrs. Nefeli Stamatiades, treasurer. In 1953, the chapter had thirty-three active members, with Mrs. Helen Yeitrakis Rousso as its president. The Chapter continued to exist thereafter, but is no longer active. The GAPA also sponsored junior orders for boys and girls ages twelve through sixteen. The junior order was founded September 17, 1950, by Supreme President of GAPA John Manos, with twin Chapters known as Orpheus for the boys and Euridoki for the girls.[33]

GAPA (Ladies' Auxiliary), circa mid-1930s. Anthousa Lodge No. 65. *First row*: Nicky Gazes, Julia P. Creticos, Celia A. Palassis, Eva A. Tsiropoulos, Anna A. Tsiropoulos, Eclecte A. Tsiropoulos, Joanna (Anna) J. Demos, Kiki G. Misoyianis, Dia G. Misoyianis, Cleo G. Kanellos, Katherine Carriott. *Second row*: Helen Eleftheroulakis, Omorfoula Skorda, Catherine Jackis, Irene M. Jackis, Elpis Vutsinas Gazes, Efterpe Tsiropoulos Stamatiades, Helen Papaharalambos, Mary Rose Palassis, Olga Milondakis, Mrs. Carriott.

GAPA (Ladies' Auxiliary), circa 1951. Anthousa Lodge No. 65. *Left to right*: Mrs. Sam M. Latto, secretary; Mrs. Peter P. Leventis Sr., president; Mrs. Olympia Giannakakides Lamis, vice-president; Mrs. Toni Manos, treasurer.

GAPA (junior order, female). *Left to right*: Lia J. Manos, Angela E. Stamas, Sophia F. Lawandales, Stephanie J. Rousso.

GAPA (junior order, male). *Left to right*: Augustine (Stino) J. Augustine, Stellios F. Lawandales, Constantine (Dino) J. Manos.

Focean Society "Elpis." *Left to right*: John T. Chakeris, secretary; Theodore C. Varras, president; John M. Rousso, vice-president; John C. Palassis, treasurer.

The GAPA ladies' auxiliary continued into 1970, when its president was Pat Gianakis Gianatos, with Corina Davoulas serving as vice-president, Effie Aliprantis Latto as secretary and Virginia Ferentinos (Peters) Manos as treasurer. The board at that time consisted of Demetra (Mitsa) Mavrantzakis Lawandales, Mary Pepergias Castanes, Marista Zira Varvalides (Varras), Helen Yeitrakis Rousso and Koula Clainos W. Lempesis.

There were other organizations like the GAPA, namely the Cephalonian Society[34] and the Asia Minor or Focean Society, with membership consisting of individuals from those locations with emphasis on their Greek heritage. The Focean Society remained in existence until at least 1951. The society, with an "Elpis" or "Hope" Chapter, was established in 1946. The entire membership consisted of individuals born in Palea Fokea, which was situated in the Gulf of Smyrna. In 1922, when war broke out between Greece and Turkey, the territory was abandoned. The population was substantially killed off. Many refugees with relatives in the United States came to this country. These groups formed the Focean Society, whose principal aim was to promote better understanding between themselves, to keep old traditions, to help distressed members and their families, to support the Greek Orthodox Church and to assist members in becoming citizens of this country. In 1951, the officers of the Charleston Chapter were as follows: Theodore C. Varris, president; John Rousso, vice-president; John T. Chakeris, secretary; and John C. Palassis, treasurer. The Board of Directors were A. Palassis, William Lefter, Fred Chacharonis, Anthony Varras and Mike Fergos.

Chapter 6

GREEK-AMERICAN/
AMERICAN-GREEK

The Greeks have always been intensely proud of their heritage, including the Greek language, customs, interest in political affairs, democratic ideals and a love for the motherland. On the other hand, the Greeks in America have also been intensely patriotic, wanting to prove themselves as good citizens of the United States. The dual emphasis of ethnicity and also being American has manifested itself not only in the history of the Greeks in Charleston, South Carolina, but also wherever Greeks migrated throughout the United States. Manifestations include the founding of the American Hellenic Educational Progressive Association (AHEPA) with its emphasis on being American, whereas the Greek American Progressive Association (GAPA) placed its emphasis on being Greek. Furthermore, this tension has existed, although diminished, in recent years, as evidenced in the debate over use of the Greek language or the English language in church services. Both languages are now assimilated into the services of the Greek Orthodox Church in Charleston.

The Greeks' intense interest in the political affairs of the motherland spilled over to Greek communities throughout the United States. In this regard, during the 1920s and up to the time war broke out in Europe with the Italian invasion of Greece in October 1940, there were heated arguments between those who supported Greece maintaining a king and a parliamentary form of government, which had been established after the Greek War of Independence, and those who supported a republic. Those in favor of maintaining a king were known as the Royalists and those supporting a Republic were called Venizelists, after Eleftherios Venizelos, who for a time served as premier or president of the Greek Republic.[35]

These arguments over Greek politics in the New World became so strident that proponents of each side split into factions affecting church and business relationships. This seems strange, but it should be noted that the early Greek immigrants maintained close ties with parents and other family members left behind in the homeland. This division manifested itself in Charleston in 1935, with two sets of officers for the Grecian Society, presently the Parish Council of the Church. The Greek grocery store owners also divided into two groups, one known as the Home Grocers and the other known as United Food Stores. Finally, when World War II broke out, unity was achieved, with everyone wholeheartedly supporting the war effort.

Chapter 7

CEMETERIES

BETHANY CEMETERY

Many early Greek settlers in Charleston are buried in Bethany Cemetery. Gregarios Papazaharia is listed as being buried there on July 1, 1918. John Schiadaressi, a cousin of Spero Schiadaressi, the second president of the Parish Council of Holy Trinity Greek Orthodox Church, is buried in Bethany with a date of death of January 29, 1912. Thomas Schiadaressi, a brother of Spero Schiadaressi, died December 16, 1915, in Augusta, Georgia, and is buried in Bethany. Thomas and John were business partners. The Schiadaressis are noted as having founded the Greek community in Augusta. An Olga Schiadaressi is buried in Bethany with a date of death of September 29, 1891, with the residence listed at Meeting and Wentworth Streets, where the Schiadaressi family resided. Another example of an early settler in South Carolina buried at Bethany is Nicholas Gazes, a brother of Chris Gazes, later president of the Parish Council of Holy Trinity Greek Orthodox Church in 1929 and 1930. Nicholas died December 19, 1916, in St. Matthews. Numerous other persons of Greek descent are buried at Bethany, with surnames such as Magoulas, Cockinos, Yeitrakis, Palassis, Misoyianis, Yatrou, Larry, Stamatiades, Ferentinos, Gianatos and Botzis. Athanasios T. Tsiropoulos, who lived to be over one hundred and was a past president of the Parish Council and a stalwart of the Greek community, was buried there more recently in 1982.

Among those interred at Bethany Cemetery are some of the pioneers of the Greek community who served on Parish Council or as officers or charter members of church or community related organizations such as the Philoptochos, AHEPA and GAPA as below listed:

Altine, Mike C. (charter member, Grecian Society)	b. Oct. 29, 1884	d. Nov. 19, 1966
Cockinos, Frank M. (charter member, AHEPA Plato Chapter No. 4)	b. Aug. 23, 1894	d. May 23, 1923
Diasourakis, Diasouris D. (AHEPA)	b. March 23, 1919	d. March 23, 1996
Ferendinos (Ferentinos), Dionysios (charter member, Grecian Society)	b. Dec. 21, 1880	d. Nov. 30, 1942
Gonos, George C. (Gounos) (charter member, AHEPA Plato Chapter No. 4)	b. 1894, Calamatos, Greece (no dates)	
Lempesis, William N. (charter member, AHEPA Plato Chapter No. 4)	b. Dec. 30, 1917	d. Feb. 27, 1980
Liatos, John P. (charter member, AHEPA Plato Chapter No. 4; Parish Council, AHEPA)	b. 1900	d. June 8, 1972
Moskos, Steve G. (AHEPA)	b. Nov. 25, 1931	d. Dec. 5, 2006
Panegeris, Frank H. (Parish Council)	b. Feb. 7, 1897	d. Nov. 21, 1965
Rousso, John M. (charter member, AHEPA Plato Chapter No. 4)	b. June 14, 1881	d. Dec. 6, 1970
Schiadaressi, Spero (charter member, Grecian Society; Parish Council)	b. July 6, 1857	d. Dec. 13, 1940
Tsiropoulos, Athanasios T. (charter member, Grecian Society; charter member, AHEPA Plato Chapter No. 4; Parish Council, AHEPA)	b. Sept. 10, 1881	d. Feb. 1, 1982
Tsiropoulos, Theodore A. (Parish Council, AHEPA)	b. Feb. 20, 1922	d. Jan. 11, 1984

Some of the information set forth above was taken from *Bethany Cemetery Inscriptions, Charleston, South Carolina*, compiled by Mildred Keller Hood for the Charleston Chapter South Carolina Genealogical Society.

On July 29, 1936, the Grecian Society purchased property at Cunnington and Skurvin Streets in Charleston County for a cemetery. This property is in proximity to Bethany and was purchased from a William F. Bresnihan for the sum of $400. Theodore Papadakos, the first president of the Parish Council of Holy Trinity Greek Orthodox Church, is buried in the cemetery together with numerous other early settlers.

As the cemetery was outgrown, a committee was formed on June 20, 1957, consisting of Elias S. Latto, chairman; Constan (Connie) J. Moskos; and Father Nicholas C. Trivelas, as appointed by the Parish Council of the church. This committee proceeded to establish a Greek section in Live Oak Memorial Gardens Cemetery, located on Highway 61. Since that time, virtually all of the deceased parishioners of Holy Trinity have been buried at Live Oak.

On Sunday, January 18, 2004, the blessing of a cemetery feature at Live Oak took place and was presided over by His Eminence Metropolitan Alexios of Atlanta, Father John G. Panagiotou and Father Nicholas C. Trivelas. The Live Oak Memorial Gardens Cemetery feature committee members were Harry G. Speliopoulos Spell, chairman; Demetrios C. Liollio, designer; Reverend John G. Panagiotou; and Reverend Nicholas C. Trivelas, Emeritus. There are four concrete benches surrounding the feature inscribed with the names of "Rev. John & Correna Panagiotou," "Father Nicholas and Despina Trivelas," "Demetrios and Caliope Liollio" and "Mary Apostle Misoyianis."

Cemetery feature at Live Oak Memorial Gardens.

OLD GREEK CEMETERY

Schedule of Plots
*** need markers on graves

Plot No.	Name	Plot No.	Name
1	Garbis, Nicholas	2	Garbis, Theodore N.
3	Arnopoulos, Irene Jackis	4	Jackis, Menelaos
5	Jackis, Katina	6	Perry, William
7	Perry, Kalleroi	8	Cargas, Diane
9-a	Cargas, James	9-b	Theos, Jerry
9-c	Chacharonis, Nick	10	Chacharonis, Fotios
11	Papadokis, Garafilis	12	Karas, James J.***
13	Boulamandis, George***	14	Kardoulas, Demetrios
15	Thomas, Haralambos***	16	Rousso, Michael
16-a	Petrakos, Jerry	17	Latto, George
18	Latto, Stamo	19	Latto
20	Kourtelis, Spero	21-a	vacant
21-b	Fergos, Tom	22	Andreatos, Andreas
23	Andreatos, Zisemos	24	Katsarakis, George
25	Panas, George	26	Magoulas, Gerasimos
27	Fludas, John	28	Fludas, Epihary
29	Stratakos, Theodore	30	Lempesis, Nicholas
31	Lempesis, Eleftheria (Ethel)	32	Zafirakos
33	Sterlakos, Stamatios	34	Croffead, Tom

Plot No.	Name	Plot No.	Name
35	Croffead, May	36	Mark, Mattie
37	vacant (outside of coping, belongs to Trapalis, Andrew)	38	Trapalis, Andrew
39	Trapalis, Alexandra	40	Trapalis
41	Diasourakis, Diasouris D.	42	Diasourakis, Constantine
43	Diasourakis, Maria	44	Manos, Julia***
45	Manos, Pete	46	Stratakos, Nick
47	Stratakos, Panagiota	48	Stratakos, George
49	Papadakos, Theodore	50	Papadakos, Demetrios
51	Christopoulos, Nick	52	Christopoulos, Hionia
53	Tsibika, Flora	54	Phillips, John
55	Phillips, George	56	Phillips, Kalliope
57	Chakeris, Evangelia	58	Christ, George
59	Christ, Chris	60	Milton, John
61	Milton	62	Katsaras, Demetrios
63	Pipergias, Christ	64	Pipergias, Zaferia
65	Diamandopoulos, A.J.	66	Diamandopoulos, Anastasia
67	Petrakis, Nick	68	Petrakis, Emma
69	Tumboli, Andrew	70	Tumboli, Litsa
71	Anagnostopoulos, Arthur	72	Anagnostopoulos, Paraskevi
73	Anastopoulo, Angelo	74	Anastopoulo
75-a	Stathius, Steve	75-b	Christophal, Dennis
76-a	Giaffis, Nick	76-b	Billias, Mike
77	Smyrniotis, Kyriakos	78	Savvas, Sam
79	Savvas, Theony	80	Savvas
81	Fergos, Lingos	82	Lingos, Stella Fergos
83	Fergos, Andronike	84	Fergos, Mike
85	Manos, James A.	86	Manos, Eva
87	Prosalentis, Jerry	88	Prosalentis
89	Magoulas, Antiope	90	Magoulas, Milton
91	Lempesis, Flora P.	92	Kontos, John
93	Kontos, vacant	94	vacant
95	vacant	96	vacant
97	Saba, vacant	98	Souad, N. El-Masarani
99	Trapales, Harry	100	Trapales, vacant
101	Pappas, Chris	102	Pappas, Betty
103	Apostolou, Persefoni	104	Nizamis, Peter
105	Nizamis	106	Logothetis, Angelo

Plot No.	Name	Plot No.	Name
107	vacant, donated to church	108	Pappas, Arthur (Papalexis)
109	Paizos/Ferentinos	110	Ferentinos, Tony
111	Paizos, Savva	112	Ferentinos, Spyro
113	Tzanatos, Alex	114	Spetseris, Nicholas
115	Takos, John	116	Takos
117	Petratos, Jerry	118	Lekas, James***
119	Pagoulatos, Triantafilos***	120	Magoulianos, Costas***
121	Grammenos, Tom***	122	Arsenis, Dennis***
123	Pappas, James	124	Likouris, J.
125	Logothetis, William J.	126	Mavronis, Demetrios
127	Chevis, Tom	128	Vlassopoulos, Steve
129	Taras, Chris	130	Hadjidemetre, Alex
131	Vasoukos, Demetre	132	Bazakas, George
133	Vasoukos, Eleftherios	134	unknown
135	Diamandoulakos, Emm.	136	unknown
137-a	Papanastasiou, Nick	137-b	Zambetis, Nick
No. ??	Gustav H. Berkha	138	Papajohn
139-a	Psaras, Gus	139	Psaras, Isidore
140	Mooneyham, Helen	141	Zoumis, Michael
142	Psaras, Evangelia Zoumis	143	Constan, Chris
144	Seregelas, Constantinos	145	Stamatakis, Emmanuel***
146	Levendelis, James	147	Galliatsatos, Speros
148	Fotinos, Panagiotis	149	Pappas, Betty***
150	Bazakas, Maria	151	unknown
152	Reizian, Sarkis	153	Fernandes, Jerry
154	Fidakis, Charles	155	Cypress, Theodore
156	unknown	157	Kefalas, Haralambos
158	unknown	158-a	Poulos, John
159	left vacant for access to water	160	Moros, Soterios***
161	Badanis, George***	162	Callas, Chris***
163	Pavlatos, Andrew	164	Derdelis, Anastasios
165	Christall, William***	166	Arfanis, George
167	Arfanis, Theodore	168	Carabatsos, George
169	Carabatsos, Stavroula	170	Corontzes, Arthur
171	Corontzes, Helen	172	Telegas, George
173	Telegas, Toula	174	Griparis, Syrmo
175-a	Glykas, Constantinos	175-b	Lawandales, Sophia A.
176	Speliopoulos, George	177	Speliopoulos, Helen

178	Philipps, Pete	179	Philipps, Olympia
180	Katsaros, Zoe		

Rosa P. Paulatos and James Demetre walked through the cemetery on June 7, 2005, and verified numbers and lots. Rosa P. Paulatos updated new burials on June 4, 2007.

LIVE OAK MEMORIAL GARDENS (GREEK ORTHODOX SECTION)

Among those interred at Live Oak Memorial Gardens are some of the pioneers of the Greek community who served on Parish Council or as officers or charter members of church or community related organizations such as the Philoptochos, AHEPA and GAPA:

Stavrides, Modestos (The Very Reverend) born Miltiades Bakalis in Epivadae, Thrace, Greece; member of the sacred brotherhood of the Holy Sepulcher; served as priest of the Greek Orthodox Church of the Holy Trinity, Charleston, SC (May 1945–May 1948); and as Priest Emeritus (1955–74)	b. Oct. 26, 1881	d. Oct. 14, 1974
Billias, George M. (charter member, Grecian Society, Parish Council)	b. 1875	d. 1978
Christ, Isidore C. (Parish Council)	b. 1926	d. Oct. 15, 1989
Croffead, Patricia Crosby (Philoptochos)	b. Nov. 14, 1946	d. Aug. 30, 1998
DeLuca, Peter D. (AHEPA)	b. Sept. 18, 1927	d. March 20, 2004
Demos, Harry P. (AHEPA)	b. 1894	d. 1979
Demos, Peter P. (charter member, AHEPA Plato Chapter No. 4)	b. 1896	d. 1960
Drake, Nicholas J. (GAPA)	b. 1898	d. 1969
Gazes, Chris D. (Parish Council)	b. Aug. 30, 1881	d. March 22, 1966
Gazes, James C. (Parish Council)	b. March 22, 1915	d. June 8, 2005
Gazes, Pat C. (Parish Council)	b. July 18, 1918	d. June 12, 2008
Gelegotis, Paul J. (Parish Council)	b. 1923	d. 2002
Gianaris, Nick H. (charter member, AHEPA Plato Chapter No. 4)	b. 1899	d. 1974
Gionis, Demetrius K. (Parish Council)	b. Nov. 26, 1896	d. Aug. 10, 1965
Hitopoulos, George (GAPA)	b. March 17, 1891	d. March 21, 1956
Hitopoulos, Harry G. (Parish Council)	b. May 26, 1926	d. May 14, 2007
Homer, Arthur S. (Art) (Parish Council)	b. 1936	d. 1986
Kambitsis, Dennis A. (Parish Council)	b. Dec. 25, 1915	d. July 19, 1992
Latto, Effie A. (GAPA, Parish Council)	b. 1906	d. May 27, 2003

Latto, Elias S. (Parish Council)	b. June 14, 1927	d. Sept. 22, 1999
Latto, Marion (AHEPA)	b. 1922	d. 2004
Latto, Sam M. (charter member, Grecian Society, Parish Council)	b. 1882	d. 1963
Lawandales, Demetra (Mitsa) Mavrantzakis (GAPA, Philoptochos)	b. 1905	d. 1985
Lawandales, Eleas F. (Parish Council)	b. 1930	d. 2003
Lempesis, Happy N., Sr. (Parish Council)	b. Dec. 14, 1927	d. May 22, 1993
Lempesis, J. Louis (GOYA, Parish Council)	b. May 15, 1919	d. March 25, 2005
Lempesis, William N. (AHEPA)	b. Dec. 30, 1917	d. Feb. 27, 1980
Logothetis, William J. (AHEPA)	b. 1897	d. 1975
Manos, Chrysanthe (Chrysa) Varras (Philoptochos)	b. Feb. 28, 1910	d. Feb. 20, 2006
Manos, George P. (GAPA)	b. 1919	d. 1976
Melissas, Andrew (Andy) L. (Parish Council, AHEPA)	b. Sept. 1, 1925	d. Sept. 18, 1987
Misoyianis, Ernest (Taso) G. (Parish Council)	b. April 20, 1921	d. Feb. 23, 1975
Morris, Margaret Gazes (GAPA)	b. 1911	d. 2003
Moskos, Marko J. (Parish Council)	b. 1918	d. 1977
Moskos, Mary Gigis (Philoptochos)	b. June 30, 1931	d. July 14, 2008
Palassis, Steve A. (Parish Council)	b. Dec. 14, 1923	d. Dec. 25, 2003
Pappas, Nicky Gazes (AHEPA, Maids of Athena)	b. 1916	d. 2007
Pavlis, Mary Poulos (Philoptochos)	b. 1910	d. 1989
Redman, Emanuel S. (AHEPA, Parish Council)	b. Jan. 28, 1927	d. Dec. 25, 1993
Speliopoulos, John G. (Parish Council, AHEPA)	b. Oct. 14, 1928	d. Jan. 15, 1989
Stoucker, Angelo E. (Parish Council)	b. June 14, 1914	d. June 20, 1988
Tellis, Anthony (Tony) J. (Parish Council, AHEPA)	b. April 7, 1928	d. July 6, 1983
Trapalis, Charles P. (charter member, AHEPA Plato Chapter No. 4)	b. 1894	d. 1965
Tumboli, Alex (charter member, AHEPA Plato Chapter No. 4, Parish Council)	b. May 21, 1900	d. May 8, 1998
Varras, Theodore C. (Parish Council, GAPA)	b. 1884	d. 1969
Vlismas, Athanasios (Tom) (Parish Council)	b. 1898	d. 1974

Some of the information set forth above was taken from *Live Oak Memorial Gardens Cemetery Inscriptions*, compiled by Nancy Hamlin Moorer for the Charleston Chapter South Carolina Genealogical Society.

Chapter 8

MISCELLANEOUS INFORMATION OF INTEREST

TOASTS TO GREEK INDEPENDENCE MADE AT HIBERNIAN SOCIETY

At the time of the War for Greek Independence, during the early 1800s, when Greece sought its freedom from the Turkish Ottoman Empire, there was great sympathy for the Greek cause in America.[36] This sympathy was reflected in Congressional resolutions supportive of the Greek cause and is found in two toasts given at St. Patrick's Day Hibernian banquets, as provided to me by Hibernian historian Donald M. Williams:

March 17, 1826
The Grecian Cause—While in America we are vainly discussing it wreaths and honor—nay Heaven once more yield it from the skies, the triumphant memorial, the Cross—*Concerto.*

March 17, 1828
Greece—Soon may her Classic soil be freed from the footsteps of the infidel and her suffering children proclaim from their native hills, the freedom of their country. *Trumpet March.*

STATE VERSUS SCHIADARESSI[37]

In Charleston in 1913, during the administration of Mayor John P. Grace, Ted Schiadaressi was charged with selling Falstaff beer in violation of the State Dispensary Act. He was arrested by Officer Jimmy Cantwell, prosecuted by City Attorney Turner

Mr. and Mrs. Ted Schiadaressi. Ted, the son of Spero Schiadaressi, is described in a 1939 yearbook of the Greek community as one of the most successful Greeks in Charleston, taking part in politics and business. He bought the entire front of Folly Island business section.

Logan, Mayor Grace's law partner, and convicted. Ted Schiadaressi was the son of Spiro Schiadaressi, the second president of the Parish Council of Holy Trinity Greek Orthodox Church. Members of the Schiadaressi family were successful businessmen in the city of Charleston.

In his charge to the jury, the trial judge explained, "I cannot, either, admit to you that we, the people of Charleston, are law-abiding. I cannot say that. I don't think there is any particular class or particular people to blame. As much as I think of and love the people of Charleston, I think they are the most lawless set there ever was."

That same year, Bishop William A. Guerry, in a powerful sermon at St. Philip's Episcopal Church, thundered that "our most respectable citizens are aiding and abetting the spirit of lawlessness in our midst (as) 'their hands are tied' through their own failure to keep the law." Charleston lawyer and historian Robert Rosen writes that the State Dispensary Act of 1893, which created a state monopoly on selling alcohol, was never really enforced in Charleston. Charlestonians ignored the state's liquor laws and continued to drink at illegal saloons called "blind tigers."

Some time after his arrest, Schiadaressi asked for the hand in marriage of Maybelle Bennett, the daughter of Charleston County jailer William J. Bennett. Permission to marry was granted on one condition—that Schiadaressi go straight—and he did so. In 1931, he opened the Folly Pier and Atlantic Pavilion, which became one of the most popular oceanfront venues in South Carolina for the next twenty-five years. Harry James, Guy Lambardo, the Inkspots and other entertainers who rode the summer circuit from New York to Miami made frequent appearances at the Pavilion.

It took much longer for other Charlestonians to "go straight." The sale of illegal spirits continued in Charleston well into the 1960s, until the passage of the mini-bottle law, a more efficient, easily regulated system of beverage control.

As for Schiadaressi, neither conviction nor politics could compel him to "go straight," but he was willing to mend his ways for the sake of love.

HUMOROUS RECOLLECTIONS

Costa Kanellos provided these recollections from his childhood attending the Greek Orthodox church in Charleston as a young parishioner.

THE FLOWERS

Every Holy Week, the women of the church used to gather to prepare the Epitaphio (Christ's sepulcher) for the special Holy Friday (Megali Paraskevi) evening service. They used hundreds of flowers, including roses and greenery, to adorn the Epitaphio and, when completed, it was a beautiful sight to behold.

In accordance with the ritual, when the Epitaphio had been brought back to the church after being carried around the block with the priest and members of the congregation following it, several men holding the Epitaphio lifted it up high so people can go under it and then reenter the church. The Epitaphio was then brought back into the church and placed in its original place, where the priest stood and began handing out flowers to the people lined up. At that point an individual began picking roses from the Epitaphio and then others started doing the same. The next thing you saw was a bunch of people yelling and grabbing flowers recklessly without regard to the priest's pleas and endeavors to restore calm. Finally, there were so many people involved that there was pandemonium and the whole Epitaphio collapsed with all the flowers strewn on the floor. In the meantime, most of the members of the congregation had fled the church.

The above occurred some time in the late 1930s.

FATHER PAPADATOS

A priest, Father Papadatos, came to Charleston in the 1930s. Mr. Kanellos remembers he was known for his rambling, sometimes incomprehensible sermons that lasted for long periods of time, sometimes causing members of the congregation to doze off.

On one particular Sunday, at the point in the liturgy when the priest says "Eirini Pasi" (Peace Be With You), Father Papadatos released a dove from the cage he had beside him. The poor dove flew up toward the ceiling, circling around the Pantocrator (Lord of the Universe), and then dove down toward the members of the congregation who, with eyes uplifted, received samples of the dove's intestines. The priest, in the meantime, tried to bring order to the laughing congregation by continuing the liturgy, but without success.

CONCLUSION

The story of the Greeks in Charleston is not unlike the histories of the French Huguenots, Germans, Irish, Italians and Jews who migrated to America. It is of note that all of the immigrant groups were proud of their ethnic heritage. Becoming Americans, however, was their number one priority. This was evidenced by the Greeks in Charleston joining organizations such as the American Hellenic Educational Progressive Association (AHEPA), wherein it was mandated that the meetings be conducted in English with emphasis on citizenship and civic endeavors. Each ethnic group endeavored to maintain its ethnic identity, but also wanted to assimilate into the Anglo-Saxon tradition of the founding fathers of this country who migrated to America predominantly from England. These histories are relevant today with respect to the migration of Mexicans to the Charleston area.

As the ethnic makeup of America continues to change, let us hope the newest immigrants can still have ethnic pride, but also assimilate as the prior immigrant groups in this country have done.

NOTES

CHAPTER 2

1. The Altine family operates the restaurant at the Charleston City Marina and has done so for many years.
2. Mr. George M. Billias was honored by the Greek community of Charleston on his 100th birthday with a resolution acknowledging his contributions to the early church in Charleston. He also founded the Greek community in Daytona Beach, Florida.
3. Also spelled Costas Christodoulopoulos.
4. Also spelled Tumboli in English.
5. Theodore Papadakos is the first president of the Grecian Society or Parish Council for the Greek Orthodox Church in Charleston.
6. Lembesis in English is Lempesis.
7. Last name also spelled Pharaclo.
8. Anthony Panayiotou.
9. The Schiadaressi brothers were some of the earliest immigrants in Charleston. They also founded the Greek community in Augusta, Georgia. The Schiadaressis were successful businessmen and one of their businesses was a fruit and confectionery store on the corner of Wentworth and Meeting Streets. Early immigrants, as told to the author by his mother, would come to Charleston and seek out the Schiadaressis for assistance obtaining employment and a place to stay. The Schiadaressis also operated a boardinghouse on the corner of King and Beaufain Streets. This building later became Dumas clothing store and is still in existence, as is the building where the Schiadaressis lived and worked on the corner of Meeting and Wentworth. The Meeting and Wentworth location, as of 2006, is known as Jestine's Kitchen. After the Schiadaressis, George D. Bazakas, a parishioner of Holy Trinity Greek Orthodox Church and a great benefactor of the church, owned the property. At one time the Stavrinakis family, who are of Greek ancestry and are members of Holy Trinity, operated a business known as the Coffee Cup at that location. One of their children, Leon M. Stavrinakis, would become chairman of Charleston County Council and a state legislator.
10. The descendants of Tom Crofead, aka Tom Croffead, have also played a prominent role in the Charleston Greek community, with Dr. George S. Croffead having served as Parish Council president during the years 1967–68. He also served the church on the Diocesan and Archdiocesan levels. Dr. Croffead is an Archon of the Greek Orthodox Church and a member of the Order of St. Andrew the Apostle. His wife, Georgia, has been very active with the church in the Philoptochos Society on the local, diocesan and archdiocesan levels. His son Thomas also served as Parish Council president in 1977.

11. Athanas T. Tsiropoulos served as president of the Parish Council of the Greek Orthodox church in Charleston for the years 1919–20 and 1946–47. He served on the Parish Council as a member in 1970–71. His son, Theodore, was also a member and officer of Parish Council. Athanas was an ardent supporter of the Afternoon School of Modern Greek and served on the School Committee for fifteen years. He would present a five-dollar gold coin to the first honor graduate of the school each year. During the 1930s, the author's mother, Margaret Gazes Morris, was awarded the five-dollar gold coin. Mr. Tsiropoulos and his family would also sponsor the annual May Day picnic for Greek school students of the community. He was an Archon of the Ecumenical Patriarch of the Greek Orthodox Church and held membership in the Order of St. Andrew the Apostle of the Greek Orthodox Church. He was the earliest person to be so honored in the community, with Dr. George S. Croffead, Dr. Peter C. Gazes and Louis (Lou) Anderson having obtained such distinctions later. Mr. Tsiropoulos lived to be over 100 years old and was honored on his 100th birthday by the Order of AHEPA Plato Chapter No. 4, of which he was president during the years 1925–26. His son Nick has further been active in the church, and both of his sons Nick and Theodore served as presidents of AHEPA Plato Chapter No. 4.

12. A descendant of Mr. Young (or Neos) has served as city attorney for the town of Mount Pleasant.

13. This statement is not accurate as to the style of the church referenced.

14. This refers to marriage between Greeks and non-Greeks, not between races.

15. Rosa P. Paulatos, Pat C. Gazes, James P. Demetre, Peter G. Morfesis and Simone Kaleondgis Alvanos provided some of the foregoing information.

16. See also article in the *News & Courier/Evening Post*, May 19, 1987, contributed by J. Douglas Donahue.

Chapter 3

17. In 1903, the Papadakos brothers (James, Theo and Stavros) began operation of a candy company at 345 King Street and resided upstairs until 1915. It was at this upstairs location that the seeds of the Grecian Society were planted, with Theodore Papadakos as the first president. Members of the Grecian Society were later known as the Parish Council of the Greek Orthodox Church in Charleston. Athanas T. Tsiropoulos operated the Crystal Ice Cream Parlor at that location from 1915 to 1916, and during this period the second floor ceased to be a residence. Later, Louis Garfield moved his jewelry business to that location in 1925, and it remained there for approximately eighty years.

18. The Grecian Society on March 10, 1951, changed its name to the Greek Orthodox Community Holy Trinity of Charleston, South Carolina.

19. Subsequent choir directors are Mary Kirlaki Pappas, Eclecte A. Tsiropoulos, Pete J. Theos, George P. Saclarides, Frances (Froso) C. Trapales (Senior Choir, Junior Choir and Male Chorus), Faye Trivelas Zoeller (Senior Choir and Junior Choir), Robert A. Henning, Leon A. Melissas (Senior Choir and Male Chorus) and Ross A. Magoulas (Junior Choir, Male Chorus, Senior Choir and Women's Choir).

20. Subsequent organists are Mary Economy, Joan Carabatsos Magoulas, Mary Drake Perry, Demetra Botzis Milam, Tula Carosatos Demetre and Diane Stamas Mashead.

21. The bouzouki is one of the oldest instruments in the history of Greek music. Its roots can be found in pre-hellenic times dating back to the ancient Egyptian, Assyrain, Chinese and Indian cultures. In classical Greece and Byzantium, we find it under the name of "pandouris" and alternately "pandoura" or "tambouras." Under Turkish denomination in more modern times, we again hear of the bouzouki in the "Demotic" songs, which were composed and sung during this period. The bouzouki is part of the popular Greek tradition because the people of Greece have sung their hopes and their sorrows with it. In modern Greek music, the bouzouki holds a similar relationship to that of the guitar in Spanish flamencos, to that of the balalaica in the Russian song and to the "Bal Musette" in popular French waltzes. The bouzouki is a string instrument made of wood, with an arm twenty-four to twenty-eight inches long and three or four pairs of chords. The versatility of the bouzouki has allowed the Greek people to express a full range of their emotions, their love of life and their love of love.

22. The property at 11 Race Street was purchased by Plato Chapter No. 4 in 1965. A dedication ceremony was held in March 1965 with Reverend Nicholas C. Trivelas conducting the dedication ceremony. Stanley E. Georgeo, president of Plato Chapter No. 4, acted as master of ceremonies. Previously, meetings were held at the Hellenic Center on Race Street. According to tax assessments, it appears that the 11 Race Street property was built in 1926. Based on its age and mode of construction, the house has historic significance.

23. The parish was without a priest from January 1936 to October 1937. Father Emmanuel Papapanagiotis performed two baptisms during this period in Charleston.

24. Schiadaressis has also been spelled Schiadaressi and Speros sometimes as Spero, Spiro and Spyro, in keeping with the difficulty of adapting names to the English language. Many of these immigrants either shortened their names or anglicized their names, as did the author's paternal grandfather. Additionally, the Greek tradition is that the first name of the father becomes the middle name of both male and female children; however, this tradition has not held fast uniformly with the Greeks in America.

25. The remaining Board of Directors in 1934 consisted of George Misoyianis, William J. Logothetis, Nick J. Bazakas, A. Palassis, Costas Moscos, James Kakaris and Isidore (Christ) Christodoulos. Honorary presidents were Theodore Papadakos and Speros Schiadaressis.

26. Paul J. Gelegotis not only served as president of Parish Council, but also was civic minded, serving in the South Carolina State legislature. His ideas and effort brought about the Emergency Medical Services to be instituted in Charleston County.

CHAPTER 4

27. Presvytera Despina Ross Trivelas provided valuable information as pertinent to the cookbook, as did Sophia Lawandales Demos and Mary Gatgounis Larry.

28. Preceding the GOYA there was the Young People's Religious Society, which was in existence in 1934 and had as its officers Ms. Viola S. Croffead, president; Ms. Julia (Chrysanthe) W. Lempesis, vice-president; Mr. Costa Campbell, secretary; and Ms. Margaret Gazes, treasurer. In 1965, the senior GOYANS organized themselves as the St. Luke's Fellowship, which in 1977 changed its name to the YAL (Young Adult League).

CHAPTER 5

29. See the *History of the Order of AHEPA 1922–1972*, by George J. Leber (1972).

30. Dr. Peter C. Gazes is the first person with Greek immigrant parents to graduate with a MD degree from the Medical University of South Carolina.

31. Dr. Elliott P. Botzis was the first graduate of The Citadel and the pharmacy school at the Medical University with Greek immigrant parents.

32. As an adult, Peter W. Lempesis was elected to Charleston City Council, where he also served as mayor pro tem during the administration of Mayor William McG Morrison. Later, he also served as a Charleston city magistrate. He was the first Greek American to be elected to public office in Charleston and also to serve in a judicial capacity.

33. There was a Juniorette GAPA organized in December 1933 that had as its officers Chrysanthe Varvalides (Varras), president; Margie S. Yiatrakis, vice-president; Margaret Gazes, secretary; and Virginia D. Peters, treasurer.

34. It is not known exactly when the Cephalonian Society was organized. In 1934, the society was known as the Society of Kefalos and had as its officers S. Schiadaressi, president; Chris Gazes, vice-president; Nicholas H. Garbis, secretary; and Antonios Magoulas, treasurer.

CHAPTER 6

35. The new airport in Athens, Greece, is named after Mr. Venizelos, and Greece no longer has a monarch.

CHAPTER 8

36. The Greek Revolution of 1821 followed the American Revolution of 1776 just forty-five years later. The slogan of the Greek liberty fighters, "Freedom or Death," reminded the American people of the famous "Give me liberty or give me death" statement of Patrick Henry. President James Monroe addressed Congress on December 2, 1822, with these words: "The name of Greece occupies our thoughts with the highest of all ideals and causes the most beautiful feelings to arise in our breasts. The memory of ancient Greece is related to art, heroism, patriotism and devotion to political freedom. The fact that such a country has been living under a grim despotic rule for centuries can only deeply sadden any proud man. Therefore, the emergence of these people fighting in the arena of liberty has naturally resulted in

enormous sympathy and emotion that is so obvious throughout our country." Many American politicians, such as President Thomas Jefferson, transmitted the popular feelings of sympathy, love and admiration for the Greek revolution in their speeches. In his speech to Congress on January 20, 1824, Kentucky Congressman Henry Clay remarked: "From Maine to Georgia, from the Atlantic Ocean to the Bay of Mexico, the acceptance has increased with lightning speed. The concern for the Greek revolution is being manifested with deep intensity; it is expressed in every form and it is increasing day by day and hour by hour." Along with political and financial support came an abundance of moral support. Americans gave Greek names to a large number of their cities, such as Ypsilanti, Ithaca, Troy, Athens, Sparta, Phoenix and others. (Excerpts from an article by John Veleris.)

37. Reprinted with the permission of William B. Regan and Frances Cantwell. William B. Regan served as city attorney under Mayor Joseph P. Riley Jr. His aunt, Maybelle Bennett, married Ted Schiadaressi.

INDEX

Please visit us at
www.historypress.net